# CITY SUGAR

## A Play

by

### STEPHEN POLIAKOFF

SAMUEL                    FRENCH

LONDON

NEW YORK   TORONTO   SYDNEY   HOLLYWOOD

# CITY SUGAR

First presented at the Bush Theatre, London, on October 9th, 1975: subsequently by Michael White at the Comedy Theatre, London, on March 4th, 1976, with the following cast of characters:

| | |
|---|---|
| **Leonard Brazil** | Adam Faith |
| **Rex** | James Aubrey |
| **Nicola Davies** | Lynne Miller |
| **Susan** | Natasha Pyne |
| **Big John** | Alan Hay |
| **Jane Harris** | Hilary Gasson |
| **Mick** | Michael Tarn |

The Play directed by Hugh Thomas
Setting by Robert Harris

The action takes place in a Sound Studio of Leicester Sound, a local commercial radio station; in the Leicester branch of a supermarket (frozen foods counter); and in Nicola's bedroom in Leicester

Time—the present

# NOTE ON THE SETTING

The main part of the action takes place in the Studio, in which the chief piece of furniture is the Sound Desk (see plan of this on p. 61). The back wall of the Studio is of plain brick. Half-way down the stage is a narrow gallery that runs right across, about eight feet above the ground. This gives access to the Control Box, set approximately c (see plan of this on p. 61). A narrow flight of stairs leads to this gallery, which can also be approached by another flight off-stage. The space below the gallery, on the opposite side from the stairs and Sound Desk, is filled in by a wall. This can be moved off, revealing a small inset in which the Bedroom and Supermarket scenes take place: the action during these scenes also making use of the stage in front of the insets.

The two small sets, Bedroom and Supermarket, are on trucks and are wheeled into position as indicated in the set plan on p. 61. Entrance to to the Studio is also possible from behind this walled section.

# CITY SUGAR*

## Scene 1

*The Studio*

*Leonard Brazil is sitting at the record desk. Rex is in the engineer's box. Pop music plays as the house lights dim, and fades after the* Curtain *rises*

**Leonard** (*into the mike*) From nineteen sixty-eight, there, Amen Corner, featuring the unmistakable soprano of Mr Andre Fairweather-Low, and "If Paradise Was Half As Nice". Welcome back to the L.B. show. L.B.—the two most important initials in the country. L.B. on five hundred and fifty waves—that's a lot of water. (*Loudly*) *Five hundred and fifty* medium waves! (*He smiles*) Sorry. "You can do better than that, Brazil." "Yes, Boss." In a few minutes we have something for you, something special. (*He begins to open the letters on the turntable desk*) I want to say hello to those I met in North Street yesterday; people out in their gardens with *green* fingers, very definitely, and green feet, too, so I'm told. And one even with green hair. No, it was very nice meeting you. They have lovely gardens up there, don't they, lovely houses! (*In his more normal voice*) I have a few letters in front of me—I've been struggling to open. I have one from Mrs Lee, Mrs D. Lee, saying that did I know there was now a topless restaurant in this fine city of ours, and its name is the Aubergine—how's that for a free commercial, you guys over there in the Aubergine—and Mrs Lee wonders, what do I think about it? I think—it's a very classy name, *The Aubergine*, perhaps in French it is something more than just a vegetable. I wonder, since we're being blue—or blue*ish*, perhaps we could ask—would any of the ladies like to see bottomless waiters approaching you with your curry? Rex is suggesting a lot of rude vegetable jokes about what that restaurant would be called, which I will ignore. Enough of this smut. I went to the cinema yesterday, saw the very excellent "Death Wish", a lot of rape and gore and blood and guts, for those of you that like your toast buttered that way—me, I prefer the lovely, the scintillating, the mind-expanding Lynsey De Paul. (*Over the beginning of the record, which he has switched on*) Nobody need fear—Lynsey De Paul is here . . . (*He turns the switch, after a few bars, the music is now playing silently while the record goes round. He drops the biro on the desk. A pause*) That was execrable. (*He flicks the intercom to speak to Rex in the box*) That was a real stinker. A loosener—and a very loose loosener at that. (*Pause; he continues into the intercom*) Come in here . . . It's the sleepy time for them at the moment, all gorged after Sunday lunch, lying in heaps

---

*N.B. Paragraph 3 on page ii of this Acting Edition regarding photocopying and video-recording should be carefully read.

round the room—they won't want to be stirred. (*Pause; louder, into the intercom*) Get yourself in here, right now!

*Rex enters behind him*

**Rex** I'm here.
**Leonard** That's better.
**Rex** I've brought a drink.
**Leonard** How kind . . . (*With a slight smile*) Trying to placate me, are you? What is it?
**Rex** Lime juice; it's a free sample of one of the commercials we're carrying this week. I thought you'd like to try it.
**Leonard** It looks like a congealed shampoo. (*He puts it to one side. Suddenly staring at Rex; loudly*) Now, why haven't you filled these up?
**Rex** I was going to.
**Leonard** Going to! Everybody keeps on telling me how efficient you are, how fortunate I am to have you. I have yet to notice. Go and do these now. (*He hands him sheets of record titles to be filled in*) I warn you, it's a particularly grisly lot. (*Smiling*) I seem to have played pap for an entire week—might as well have stuck the stylus into cotton-wool.

*Rex moves slightly*

And why hasn't my mail been checked . . .?
**Rex** (*embarrassed*) Sorry, I . . .
**Leonard** (*holding up a letter*) I've been asked to open another municipal pleasure pond—which is completely out of the question, of course.
**Rex** Why?
**Leonard** (*riffling through his other letters*) The last time—the one and only time I had to baptize a pond—it was in front of councillors and crowds, and all the rest—and I had to launch it—with a champagne bottle, containing—(*suddenly looking up*)—and this is completely and utterly true—frog spawn. A bottleful. I wasn't allowed to smash it against the side, of course, I had to solemnly pour it out, and of course the bloody stuff got stuck and I had to stand there shaking it, and banging the bottom, like a ketchup bottle, until, of course, I got it all over myself. (*He looks up*) What I really hate is somebody that doesn't believe a good true story. (*Loudly*) Get on with it!

*Rex moves slightly*

(*Loudly*) What's more, I've never seen a single person even *near* that pond—thousands of pounds spent on a small, windswept hole in completely the wrong place.
**Rex** I—By the way—I've left an item there—(*indicating the desk*)—you might like.
**Leonard** You have, have you? Worse and worse, Rex. You're having a good day, aren't you? (*Smiling*) I don't like suggestions very much, you should know that by now.

**Rex** Yeah, but I thought—you could—I wanted . . .
**Leonard** No!

*Rex exits*

(*He turns suddenly to the mike, turns on a record over the monitor speakers and fades it down*) That was Miss De Paul. I'm now struggling with another letter on pink paper—it's from Mrs Joan Parsons saying "Dear Leonard, is it true or false that you were a teacher in another life?" Well, now, I don't know about another life, Joan, but I was in this one, yes. I trained as a teacher as it happens, before I slipped into the record business, and when all that went up in a puff of smoke, I slipped back into the classroom, until of course I heard the call of Leicester Sound. I thought that everybody knew that, Joan. (*Smiling*) A joke. And a note here from a theatre group calling itself the Gracious Prayers, saying, could I give a free plug to their production of Dame Agatha Christie's *Towards Zero* on Saturday at the Town Hall, Hinkley, which seats one thousand five hundred people. No wonder they wanted their free mention. And I'm now being handed by the ever-dependable Rex, a piece of paper on which is written "DON'T FORGET". And if you don't know what that means, I do, and I'll tell you in a moment, for we have a real thriller coming up; but to change the subject—(*putting on a record*)—I have lost some weight. In fact I've lost so much weight, I'm floating out of my seat, floating round the studio. (*Ghost-story medium voice*) They've had to weigh down my trousers with *Encyclopaedia Britannicas*. (*In his normal voice*) While our friend Rex is gaining all the time, I'm afraid, he's approaching sixteen stone now, a hunky piece of flesh, can hardly fit into his box. Enough of this gibberish. DON'T FORGET means competition time. We have a stunner for you in a moment—till then, let's flash back into the dim distant past of last week. (*He switches on a record, "It's Gonna Sell A Million"; he turns it off after a couple of bars*) That was better—that was very slightly better. (*He gets up and walks*)

*Rex enters*

**Rex** Why do you keep on doing this?
**Leonard** Doing what?
**Rex** You know . . .
**Leonard** Putting weight on you, you mean—making you an obese lump. It's my rather dismal little joke.
**Rex** I thought—you were the one for truth over the air.
**Leonard** I allow myself this one slight distortion.
**Rex** But people will discover, won't they?
**Leonard** No they won't, nobody's ever going to publish a picture of you, are they?
**Rex** Yes. (*Pause*) The local press might.
**Leonard** (*smiling*) Not with shares in this station they won't. In fact a

total wall of silence could be preserved about your real size for ever-more. In fact if I wanted I could pump you up steadily to twenty-five stone, and then burst you. (*Pause*) Sorry. (*Smiling*) Don't worry, I do it to everyone that works for me.

**Rex** So I've heard.

**Leonard** So there's no need to look injured. You're not, yet.

*Rex moves to go*

**Rex** (*with a slight smile*) By the way, I've got Capitol on the line.

**Leonard** (*without looking up*) You'll have to be more convincing than that. Been listening to jabber and gossip, have you?

**Rex** I suppose so, yes.

**Leonard** Well don't.

**Rex** (*watching him*) Everybody knows, anyway. Are they going to make an offer, then?

**Leonard** It's just possible. Everything's possible. I shouldn't bank on it.

**Rex** For the afternoon show . . . (*Smiling*) They'll be sending spies up here. They'll be sitting in pubs with transistors and earplugs, listening away. You'll have to give them the whole works.

**Leonard** (*not looking up*) Will I . . . Get it ready.

**Rex** It is ready.

**Leonard** (*totally matter-of-fact*) You can have a moment longer than usual, because I'm in a generous mood.

**Rex** Thanks—I——

**Leonard** (*cutting him off, swinging round to the mike and switching on the monitor speakers; fading down the end of the record*) And now, a special competition. You heard me—a mind-tingling competition. And by my side is the ever-dependable Rex, sweating slightly, what have we got as a prize, Rex?

**Rex** (*nervously, standing by the mike and speaking into it; putting on almost a BBC voice*) We have *their* latest LP—the Yellow Jacks' latest!

**Leonard** (*in a brash voice*) Tell us the title, Rex—*please* tell us the title.

**Rex** "Somewhere Up There."

**Leonard** That's a fine title—is it a fine record?

**Rex** It's very exciting, Leonard, it really is . . .

**Leonard** (*to the listeners*) And you can have it a whole two or three weeks before it's in the shops, one of the very first in the whole country to have it. And what is Rex going to make us do? Well, I think he's been fiddling with his tapes.

**Rex** I have indeed . . .

**Leonard** Very posh today, aren't we, Rex?

**Rex** Are we, Leonard?

**Leonard** And what have you done with your tapes?

**Rex** I've slowed them down—rather a lot.

**Leonard** Slowed them down—we're getting even more posh.

**Rex** Yes.

**Leonard** (*loudly*) Tell me, Rex, what affect does this have on the listener?

**Rex** What?

**Leonard** (*very fast*) What effect does this have on the *listener*?

**Rex** What—well it . . . (*He dries completely and stands helpless*) I . . .

*Leonard presses a button: a tape of Leicester Sound jingle cuts off Rex's floundering. Rex returns to his box*

**Leonard** Enough of this gibberish. (*In his normal voice*) O.K., sweets—this is it. Rex is going to play one of the songs in the Top *Eleven*, and it has been sl-o-o-o-owed do-o-o-own, so it sounds a little different. And you're going to give us the singer and the song, aren't you. Double-five-three-zero-four—is the number to ring—that's right. (*In a Bogart voice*) Play it again, Rex.

*Rex, back in his box, switches on a tape of "The Proud One" by the Osmonds, at 16 r.p.m.*

(*after a few bars, reducing the volume on the monitor speakers; talking into the intercom to Rex; off the air*) Sounds a little more exciting like this, doesn't it. I shall always play it like this in future. (*Suddenly, loudly*) All records will be played at *eight* R.P.M., and we'll talk that slowly, too.

*Rex comes out of the box*

**Rex** I'm—I'm sorry about messing things up, I didn't mean to . . .

**Leonard** Of course you didn't . . .

**Rex** You took me by surprise, I didn't think . . . I'm sorry, I won't do it again.

**Leonard** No, of course you won't. You won't get another chance to. Now get back into your box where you belong.

*Rex returns to the box. Leonard switches the mike to go live again, and speaks loudly*

Rex—what have you done to my favourite song? How's that for first-degree murder—a fine song slo-o-o-owly tortured to death. O.K., sweets, who can be the first caller—race to your phones, dial furiously. I'm touching the first prize now—all fourteen tracks of it—we're handling the two of them with rubber gloves up here—and forceps, and we're keeping them in an incubator at night, in case we can hatch a third. Seriously now—(*he puts headphones on*)—we have a caller; and the first caller is . . .

**A Girl's voice** (*on the telephone, amplified through monitors*) Hello . . .

**Leonard** (*softly*) Hello there—what's your name, love?

**Girl** Angela.

**Leonard** Lovely. Have we ever talked before?

**Angela** No, never.

**Leonard** Fine. You at home, Angela?

**Angela** Yeah—I'm at home.

**Leonard** Good—well, let's go straight into it, Angela, into the unknown . . .

*He signals to Rex, who switches on the slowed-down tape again, in the background*

Who do you think the noise is, this *slo-o-ow* noise?
**Angela** Is it—"The Proud One" by the Osmonds?
**Leonard** Did you say . . .
**Angela** (*about to correct herself*) I——
**Leonard** (*interrupting*) Angela, you're r-r-r-o-o-o-ight! Well done!

*Rex speeds up the record to the right speed; it plays a few bars; Leonard signals to Rex and the volume is reduced*

There we go—clever girl. I'm dropping your prize into Rex's hand, to be wiped spotless, and posted, jet-propelled, towards you, Angela. 'Bye, love. Let's have the next one, Rex.

*A slowed-down version of "Na Na Is the Saddest Word" by the Stylistics. Leonard gets up again. Rex comes out of the box*

This is an easy kill for them—they use their record-players so much at home, they all run slow anyway—those who *have* record-players.
**Rex** (*staring at Leonard*) I really like it, you know—(*with a slight smile*)—*if* I'm allowed to say so, how you always touch something when you're talking about it, even if it's the wrong record, like just now. (*He returns to the box*)
**Leonard** Yes. I like that, too. It's the actor in me. It's what makes it reasonably good. (*Staring round the studio*) Where is the nauseating object, anyway? (*He sees the Yellow Jacks' L.P. and picks it up*) Have you read the back, with Ross—(*in an American film-trailer voice*)—the leader singer speaking *his mind*—(*in his normal voice*)—take an example at random—and this is a nice lad from Bolton speaking—"Ross numbers among his favourite things; walnut ice-cream, honeysuckle, genuine people, starfish, and sunburnt bare feet." (*Loudly*) You realize we're going to have to play the utterances of this jellied imbecile all this week— the promoters have sent us a long tape, in a silk case, and the station's excited, too, they want it to be a lively few days, I keep getting little illiterate messages pushed under the door saying "Please remember, *maximum* required". (*Switching on the mike suddenly*) Hello—what's your name, please?
**A Girl's Voice** Rita.
**Leonard** (*with a slight smile*) Lovely Rita Meter Maid.
**Rita** What?
**Leonard** A reference to years gone by, don't let it worry you, Rita. Have we talked before?
**Rita** No.
**Leonard** You listen often . . .
**Rita** Yes—yes I do.
**Leonard** (*smiling, softly*) Good, that's how it should be. Let's go straight into it then, love, into the nitty-gritty—who do you think it is?
**Rita** I think it's "Whole Lot of Loving" by Guys and Dolls. (*She gives the wrong title*)
**Leonard** Well, Rita, you're wrong, I'm afraid.
**Rita** No I'm not—am I?

**Leonard** I'm afraid so.

**Rita** You sure? (*Louder*) I was certain. You——

**Leonard** (*cutting her off*) I'm sorry, love, you're wrong; keep listening though, for a very important reason—'bye for now. (*In a Hughie Green voice*) And let's go straight on to the next contestant! Coming up to Big John with the news at three o'clock. One down, one L.P. to go—round, crisp and shiny. What's your name, please?

**Nicola's Voice** Hello

**Leonard** A little louder please—what's your name?

**Nicola** (*very quietly*) Nicola Davies.

**Leonard** A little louder.

**Nicola** (*loudly*) Nicola Davies.

**Leonard** Nicola Davies. That's very formal. Are you at home, Nicola Davies?

**Nicola** Yes.

**Leonard** And what are you wearing, Nicola?

**Nicola** I—trousers . . .

**Leonard** A little louder—you've got a very nice voice, Nicola. You're wearing trousers; and anything else?

**Nicola** Yes—shoes.

**Leonard** Shoes, that's an interesting picture, she's wearing just trousers and shoes. Only wish we had television phones, sexy Nicola—so, to win this L.P., that Rex is just slipping into its beautiful see-through, tight-fitting sleeve—who is it, Nicola?

**Nicola** It's the Stylistics and "Na Na is the Saddest Sound". (*She gives the wrong title*)

**Leonard** I'm afraid, Nicola——

**Nicola** (*interrupting, correcting herself*) No, it's "The Saddest Word".

**Leonard** Well, Nicola—I'm afraid your first answer is the only one I can accept . . .

**Nicola** Oh . . .

**Leonard** But you were very close—and so, as you've given us *all* your name, Nicola Davies—I'm going, actually, to give it to you.

**Nicola** Oh good—thank you.

**Leonard** Just for you, Nicola Davies, but on one condition—and that is . . .

**Nicola** (*nervously*) What is that?

**Leonard** You listen for just one more moment, because I have something rather extraordinary to announce to you and to everyone. I'm going to be running many competitions this week for all ages—but one of them is different—for, to tie in with the great Yellow Jacks' concert here in this city on Saturday—we're running THE COMPETITION OF THE CENTURY—and the prize is actually meeting one of the boys. How do you like that, Nicola Davies?

**Nicola** Yes—what do you do?

**Leonard** And not only that—the winner will ride to London, after the concert, in *their* car, sitting with *them*, and what is more they will then spend four whole days in London, the capital of this fine country, at the expense of Leicester Sound. That's O.K., isn't it, Nicola?

**Nicola** Yes—what do——

**Leonard** (*cutting her off*) So everybody tune in tomorrow, for the first
stage—you too, Nicola—(*smiling*)—you never know—what your luck
might be. We might even speak again. (*He puts down the phone and drops
his biro on the desk*)

*Pause. Quiet*

We're off.

*The Lights fade to a Black-out*


Scene 2

*A commercial is heard on the soundtrack*

**A Sharp Transatlantic Voice** We are going DOWN! DOWN! DOWN!
Yes, everything's down at Liptons. Shop at Liptons where eggs are
down—(*echoing*)—DOWN! DOWN! Bacon is down and what's not
down's not up.

**Song** Liptons makes the going easy,
   Liptons makes the going great!

*As the song continues there is a sudden explosion of white Light—*

*The Supermarket. The music of the commercial breaks into pop music
playing in the background. Nicola is standing by a refrigerator, staring
ahead; her face is pale. She has a postcard in her hand*

**Susan** (*off*) Nicola?

*Nicola doesn't react*

   *Susan enters*

   Nicola? Here . . .

*Nicola glances up, and suddenly Susan crosses over to the refrigerator, very
sharply*

**Nicola** (*surprised; nervously*) What you doing over here?
**Susan** What do you think?
**Nicola** You shouldn't have come over. You know you're meant to stick
to your own counter.
**Susan** Why should I? I hate standing over there, by myself all the time.
I've got to talk to somebody, haven't I—even you! Anyway, I start
thinking funny thoughts, after a bit. (*She glances up at the strip-lighting*)
If you stare at those lights long enough, it does that.
**Nicola** (*sharply*) You'll be seen any moment, you know.
**Susan** I won't. (*She feels her tunic*) Christ, I'm tired after that rush, and

it'll soon be starting again. I get so hot in this—(*pulling at the tunic*)—
all over. What's that—let's see that . . .?
**Nicola** Nothing.
**Susan** (*making a grab for it*) What you got a postcard for, with nothing on it.
**Nicola** Stop it! You'll get it wet. (*She puts the postcard back*) Look, if
I'm seen talking to you, by the camera—(*they both glance up*)—we'll
both get it, won't we? You just have to make a wrong move, and he'll
see you, won't he?
**Susan** Don't worry, I'm watching out. (*She smiles*) It's coming now. (*She
ducks*) You know what happened yesterday? Something exciting. What
do you think—a cat got in here, it did. Just after you'd gone. Came
through the stacks of Rivita up there, suddenly there it was. IN HERE!
You know, spitting and everything. I thought it was a giant rat, we all
suddenly stopped what we were doing and rushed after it, shouting and
screaming our heads off. It really got everybody going. You should have
seen us. Made a change. Didn't last long—you missed it!
**Nicola** Yes.
**Susan** (*loudly*) I wonder if anything else will get in here soon.
**Leonard's Voice** (*suddenly piping up*) That was . . . Don't fear, Leonard
Brazil is here. Hello there, wherever you are, whatever you're doing,
and a special hello to you. (*As if to all the girls, but strangely personal*)
Yes, you down there, I'm saying hello to you.
**Nicola** He's quite loud today.
**Susan** Yes, he is.
**Leonard's Voice** (*running on*) I've got a lot of goodies coming up, and no
bad 'uns. Every sound is freshly picked up here, specially for you,
that's why they're so ripe and full of flavour. Juicy! You don't believe
me, well, it's true.

*Music begins*

**Susan** He's talking a lot today, isn't he?
**Leonard's Voice** Very soon that special something I promised, Stage
One . . .
**Nicola** Yes.
**Leonard's Voice** Until then, let's move on to the year two thousand and
maybe we'll be listening to this.

*Music: "Long-Haired Lover from Liverpool"*

**Susan** (*looking into the refrigerator*) I'm so hungry, aren't you, can't stop
feeling hungry.
**Nicola** Careful what you're doing. He'll kill us if he sees.
**Susan** (*putting her hand inside the refrigerator*) It's horrible inside here.
We could fuse this fridge, you know—just have to get the right thing.
(*She pulls at something inside the refrigerator*) Once saw it happen, all the
food melts slowly, goes soggy and bad, and it all floats in a big kind of
mush, you can pour the whole lot out like a lot of soup. (*She pushes
the refrigerator*) It moves, too, you see!
**Nicola** Don't, please. I don't want trouble today, Susan . . .

**Susan** (*pushing the refrigerator*) It moves easily, we could push it down
there if we wanted.
**Nicola** (*shouting*) Mind!

*Susan springs back as the camera pauses*

(*Nervously*) He's seen us now. Think. You're going to get us sacked at
any moment now.
**Susan** I wouldn't mind that—I wouldn't. Anyway, he's asleep most of the
time, the guy who watches it. Up in the office.
**Nicola** No, he's not! When there aren't many customers, like now, he's
watching us all the time.
**Susan** Yes, he enjoys doing that. It's his sort of game. Come on! (*She
calls to the camera, then ducks*)
**Nicola** Have you seen him yet? Do you know what he looks like?
**Susan** Yes, I saw him through the door once. He's very fat. I've heard
all about him, he sits there all day, with one of his socks off, picking his
toes, and eating the stuff, while he watches.
**Nicola** He doesn't do that, does he?
**Susan** Yes—he used to be a policeman, you know. And when he sees a
customer taking something or one of us, he has them up there, and he
says "he'll let them go". If he can do what he likes with them for half
an hour, put his hand down you know and that. (*She mimes it*)
**Nicola** You're making all this up, like always.
**Susan** I'm not. It's true! And that's why you stare so much at the camera,
isn't it? Because you wanted to get noticed—be invited up there. You
want that to happen, don't you?
**Nicola** I don't. Well, it might be interesting. But I don't just wonder about
him!
**Susan** Maybe he's staring at us, right at this moment, smacking his lips—
about to jump. (*She looks into the refrigerator*) Have you taken anything
yet, then?
**Nicola** No.
**Susan** Have you stopped taking things, then?
**Nicola** No, but they've started searching us, haven't they?
**Susan** Yes. My mum doesn't believe they search us. She can't think why
they should have to, except for bombs, in case we had bombs! (*She puts
her hand in the refrigerator*)
**Nicola** It's coming round again. Careful!
**Susan** Nicola—let's take something now, right now.
**Nicola** (*astonished*) What?
**Susan** Come on—take that! (*She throws Nicola a packet of food*) And that
—and that! (*She throws a huge bundle of food from the refrigerator at
Nicola*)
**Nicola** Look, stop it, Susan. Stop it, it's coming . . .!

*A large can drops out of her hands and rolls down stage. At the same moment
the music cuts off. Silence. Nicola turns, frightened, bewildered, and rushes
out in front of the refrigerator to pick up the can*

**Ross's Voice** Don't move, folks, stay right where you are, because yes, it's me. See you Saturday.

**Leonard's Voice** Those few words were spoken by you know who, Ross. I'll be playing some more of his dulcet tones tomorrow.

**Nicola** Shhh! I want to really listen now.

**Leonard's Voice** (*strangely gentle, as if half-aimed at her*) So have you got a lead pencil ready—is it in your hand—are you gripping it—hold it—tight—won't you, because we've come to that moment you've been waiting for since yesterday . . .

**Susan** (*loudly*) You're not going in for that competition, are you, you can't . . .

**Nicola** Sssh! Be quiet,

**Leonard's Voice** Come on, now then, are you ready, because I'm only going to say it *once*, so pin back those ears of yours, and listen—ready . . .

*Sudden silence*

**Nicola** (*loudly*) What's that . . .?

*Just silence*

They've switched it off.

**Susan** (*smiling, teasing*) Yes—they must have known what you were going to do.

**Nicola** They would switch it off then!

**The Fat Man's Voice** (*silky, nauseating, menacing*) Attention all staff. Can Miss Lyle come into the office please. Could Miss Lyle come here immediately, please—immediately . . .

**Susan** (*loudly, defiantly*) It's not us—it's that old bag, seen her nicking . . .

**Nicola** (*moving backwards and forwards*) They were only going to say it once, weren't they? How can I find it out?

**Susan** You can't go in for *that* competition. You won the record yesterday. They wouldn't even let you start.

**Nicola** I must find it out, probably won't be something like this for ages—where's the building that it comes from?

**Susan** No idea. They'd never let you in, either.

**Nicola** No. (*She turns*) I'll phone them up, then. I know the number.

**Susan** (*smiling*) Can't use that phone. Only for supervisors.

**Nicola** I don't care. (*She moves towards the phone*)

**Susan** (*loudly*) Mind! Nicola!

*The camera stops—and pauses*

You'll never get over there without being seen. He's watching now.

*Nicola stares at the phone*

**The Fat Man's Voice** Miss Lyle . . .

**Nicola** It's worth a try. I'm going to. (*She moves in front of the refrigerator, sideways, crouches, dashes furiously for the phone, pauses for one second,* *then she immediately starts dialling furiously, bending to keep her head down)*

**Susan** (*calling across*) Keep down . . . down. You haven't got long now. Hurry!

*A very loud engaged tone is heard, Nicola slams the phone down, then immediately starts again*

Probably hundreds of people trying—everybody. You won't get to speak to *him* again.

**Nicola** Sssh!

*The very loud engaged tone is heard. Nicola slams down the receiver, then immediately starts again*

**Susan** It's coming round, Nicola.

*Nicola dials furiously*

You're going to get seen!

*Nicola glances up and freezes as the camera passes*

It's on you!

**Nicola** (*staring up*) Go away! (*She finishes dialling*)

*Very loud pips are heard*

I hate that noise. (*She moves back to the refrigerator, not caring if she is seen or not*)

**Susan** There you are. I told you.

**Leonard's Voice** (*suddenly piping up*) What about that, then? What did you think of that. Souper, dooper as they say in Russia. That was only the start, remember, wasn't it?

**Nicola** It would happen, wouldn't it?

**Leonard's Voice** Of course I've been asked to repeat it, say it again for *you* that weren't listening. Yes—I mean you. Which is against the rules, and I'll probably be fined an enormous sum of money and get banned for life, but I'm going to, just for you.

**Nicola** Hear that?

**Leonard** O.K., love. Here's stage one again. The First Great Stage, and it is, if you could go anywhere in the world you can think of, with one of the Yellow Jacks, which one would you choose, where would you go, and why. (*In a jokey voice*) You're not allowed to choose me, and the *thirty* best ones get through to stage *two*. That's not so difficult, is it, in fact it's the easiest I could make it for you—isn't it? And now . . .

*Music starts: Leonard cues a record*

**Susan** Now you know, don't you?

**Nicola** Yes, leave me alone now.

**Susan** Your postcard's filthy, you know.

**Nicola** Yes, but I can still write on it, can't I?

**Leonard's Voice** Are you O.K., then? It's over to you.

*The music comes up loud*

I'm waiting for you, aren't I?

*The music becomes louder still, as the Lights fade to a Black-out*


SCENE 3

*The Studio*

*Leonard Brazil is standing by his desk. A record is playing silently. A spool of tape is going round, and we hear Leonard's personal jingle over the speakers: "L.B. . . . L.B. . . . L.B. . . . L.B. . . . L.B. . . . L.B. . . ." He turns the volume up. "L.B. . . . L.B. . . . L.B. . . ."*

*Mick, a seventeen-year-old youth with a nervous manner, drags in four sacks bulging with postcards. Leonard flicks off the jingle and swings round*

**Leonard** What are you doing with those?
**Mick** (*nervously*) I—I'm carrying them in here, Mr Brazil.
**Leonard** Nothing is allowed in here, you know that.
**Mick** Yes—Mr Brazil.
**Leonard** (*staring*) What are they?
**Mick** (*very nervously*) They're bags. I . . .
**Leonard** Yes?
**Mick** Replies from the listeners. Rex is finishing sorting them—you see—and they're so many we thought you'd like to see them.
**Leonard** (*casually*) Did you. (*He puts his hand into one of the bags, and pulls out some postcards*) All these are replies, are they?
**Mick** You really got them to write in all right, didn't you—Mr Brazil.
**Leonard** (*with a slight smile*) I had a ridiculous dream about these girls last night, do you know that?
**Mick** (*nervously*) No—Mr Brazil.
**Leonard** (*lightly*) I was in a small park. There was a whole line of them coming towards me—about twenty of them, and they said they wanted to give me a present—a new pair of trousers, but could they first have my old ones to burn. They must have my old ones to burn immediately. (*He looks at Mick*)
**Mick** (*bewildered*) Yes?
**Leonard** (*turning sharply, businesslike*) Come on, take these all out again—the whole lot at once.
**Mick** (*struggling to pick them up*) Yes, of course.
**Leonard** This place is meant to be the nerve centre of the City, isn't it. And you fill it with all this clobber. Go on, we have very little time. (*He brings up the record and goes on the air*)

*Rex enters, stops Mick picking up the bags, and they both stand and watch Leonard from the side*

No need to fear. I'm here again. And now I've got something to say, folks. (*In a gentle tone*) To all of you, I have a message from our little friends, the PO-Leese. They say a lot of people in this fine city of ours have been taking what doesn't belong to them. In plain full frontal language, STEALING, and our little friends in blue have had to go into schools and shops, and put down the deadly purple dye—so they can catch them, purple-handed. So seriously now, I know times are hard, but keep out of trouble—you will, won't you? (*His tone changes*) Very soon on this Wonderful Wednesday we have Big John with all the News In The World—till then, let's explode with a raving cataclysmic ditty from nineteen sixty-eight, the Rolling Stones and "I Can't Get No Satisfaction".

*There is an explosion of sound*

*Mick leaves silently*

*Leonard listens to the music for a moment, then sees Rex and cuts the sound suddenly*

What you doing?

**Rex** (*standing, staring*) I was watching you.

**Leonard** That's not permitted, especially the amount you do. Your ogling is getting on my nerves. Why do you do it?

**Rex** Because it really interests me, doesn't it. (*He smiles*) Have you heard anything from Capitol? (*Quickly*) Do you think they're listening now and going to——

**Leonard** (*sharply*) That, Rex, is a forbidden subject, and you know it is. Come on, we have three minutes to go.

**Rex** (*still standing there*) Yes, Leonard—I wondered if—I just happen to have an item here I thought you might like or perhaps even . . .

**Leonard** You could have a quick spot and read it yourself? That's what you were going to say, wasn't it? You're pushing, aren't you, lad. I do believe you're beginning to *push*. I've never ever seen somebody begin so early.

**Rex** I'm not . . . I—(*quickly*)—I'll just read it, shall I? (*He takes out a black notebook*)

**Leonard** That's the little notebook with all of Rex in it, that you keep hidden in your box.

**Rex** It's an absurd news item. (*He reads*) "And we've just heard that in a Wall's factory in Luton, a severed leg was found in a vat of raspberry ripple ice-cream. The authorities are checking to see if they've got a cone big enough for it."

*Silence*

**Leonard** Even from somebody like you, that is quite diabolically dreadful. You're a disgrace to this microphone. (*He suddenly looks him straight in the face*) You are!

**Rex** (*startled*) What do you mean? What's wrong with it? People like black jokes now—I've some *much* blacker ones, you know. They love them—can't have enough. It's what they really want.

**Leonard** (*suddenly*) You don't have to tell me what they want, Rex.

**Rex** No, of course not. (*With genuine admiration; quietly*) I know *you* know.

**Leonard** That's better.

*Big John enters; a shiny, red-faced man. He carries a file*

**John** Hello, there, everyone. (*Smiling*) Two minutes to go.

**Leonard** The lad's being pushy.

**John** Is he? That's no surprise.

**Rex** (*suddenly nervous*) I'm sorry, I didn't mean . . .

**Leonard** We've got to go on to Stage Two in two minutes. Go on—get out!

*Rex exits*

(*He switches on to the air without a break, fading the record*) Hello, sweets—stand by. Very soon now you'll have you know what. Till then, here's . . . (*He plays something very cheap and nasty. As soon as he is faded out he swings round and cuts back like lightning into his talk with Rex, who has gone. Loudly*) And you make one mistake, Rex, and you're fired. (*To John, more quietly*) That boy makes me nervous.

**John** I didn't know that was possible.

**Leonard** (*flicking round, staring at John*) You look particularly cheerful today, don't you, John?

**John** Thank you. I'm in very good form, yes.

**Leonard** As usual, you've probably got a train disaster and a couple of mass murders there—(*he taps John's file*)—and your cheeks are positively glistening—Bright and Rosy.

**John** Thank you. (*Smiling*) But I haven't got anything really spectacular now—maybe by teatime something will come in.

**Leonard** (*with a slight, teasing smile*) Good.

**John** What's this I've just heard about approaches from the Big Wide World, from the actual Capitol Radio. Are they going to . . .?

**Leonard** You didn't hear anything of the kind. (*Loudly*) *Nothing* of the KIND!

**John** (*startled*) I'm sorry, I didn't realize . . .

**Leonard** No, you don't, John. You see this. (*He picks up a piece of paper*) This piece of paper—*that is the competition of the century.* (*He holds it up*)

**John** (*looking at it*) Yes, it's a real cash box week, this week, isn't it? One minute, fifteen seconds to go . . .

**Leonard** And you know what . . . (*He pauses*) I've done something which I've never done before, John. I've picked out an average girl for this competition. Yes, I picked out her voice. I home in on her each time I go on the air, home in on that voice. And imagine her face. It would be funny if she knew, wouldn't it?

**John** (*hardly looking up*) Really?

**Leonard** In fact, each time I pass by the window, I half expect to see her—
a small dot standing right down there, staring up towards here, her
spectacles flashing—if she wears spectacles. (*He glances at John, not
listening*) You're the only one that knows yet, *John*.

**John** Yes. I've got no tongue-twisters today, luckily. One minute to zero.
Peppermint? (*He sucks one himself*)

**Leonard** If there was an earthquake today or a full-scale revolution those
girls wouldn't notice, not a chance. (*Abrasively*) I taught kids that age
once, years ago! But they weren't like this. (*He taps John's file*) Got any
earthquakes locked in there?

**John** No, thank goodness. Nothing like that.

**Leonard** Perhaps you should have.

**John** (*suddenly looking up*) You must be enjoying all this anyway—it's
your greatest week ever, isn't it?

**Leonard** Oh, I am. I am.

**John** After all, you've always been wonderful at whipping people up,
getting them to TUNE IN. You only have to say the word . . .

**Leonard** Yes?

**John** Just have to breathe over the air. They're all waiting for you now.

**Leonard** (*standing over the controls*) That's right, John. Got your little
furry mascot ready, have you? Go on, *hold it up*!

**John** (*holding up a furry mascot so Leonard can see*) Yes, of course I have.
Ten seconds to zero . . .

**Leonard** You dropped it yesterday in mid-sentence. Hold on to it very
tightly, John. (*He flicks on a switch and fades out the music*) That was
the very savage sound of . . . (*His tone changes and becomes personal*)
We're coming to you very soon now, so don't fret, don't worry. It's
three o'clock and here's Big John with all the News In The World.

*John starts reading the news, world items of extreme unrest, mingled with
local items. As he reads, Leonard moves to the far end of the studio, out of
microphone range, and calls out remarks to him, trying to put him off*

(*Smiling*) You know, John, I don't seem to be able to believe anything
you say today. I'm talking through your news, John. I think your
mascot's going to fall. (*He moves back to John*) Perhaps you need a
tickle.

*Leonard goes to John, who is reading the news unwaveringly, and begins to
tickle him under the chin, then under the arms, in the ribs. John shifts in his
chair, but keeps reading*

(*Sharply, going to his desk*) It's got no life in it.

**John** (*on the air*) And now back to Leonard, and that competition of the
century.

**Leonard** Our thanks to Big John for reading the news so nicely and so
firmly. Stand by, love, any moment. (*Music plays. He fades it down:
"Herb Alpert"*)

**John** Somebody'll hear you one day, Leonard. Always jealous of people taking away your microphone, aren't you—even for a moment. Always trying to put them off . . .

**Leonard** Rubbish! Anyway, I never manage to . . . (*Suddenly he becomes really abusive*) *Competitions have an effect on me!*

*Rex enters suddenly and loudly with a trolley completely smothered in objects*

**Rex** Here you are!

**Leonard** (*facing him*) What are those?

**Rex** They're your bribes.

**Leonard** (*sharply*) My what?

**Rex** Your bribes, Leonard—from the girls.

**Leonard** (*completely surprised*) They sent all those? Why?

**Rex** (*scrambling over the trolley*) They're hundreds of them—a watch, nicked from her dad, probably—a "T" shirt with your initials on it, some cheese, some socks with toes, a whole cake with *you* on it, a walking-stick, and lots of photos of themselves.

**Leonard** (*quietly, staring at the trolley*) All for me . . .? (*He picks up the photos and stares at them*)

**John** (*moving over to the huge stack of bribes*) You're doing very well out of this, aren't you? I don't know what you're worrying about. You're in the middle of a glorious week. (*He begins feeling objects and pawing through them*) We've never had a response like this. Could live off this for a month. (*Casually*) I wonder if there's anything there for me. (*He picks up the watch, or the cheese*) I could do with this. (*He pockets it*)

**Leonard** John! Go and find some more *News*. Something worth listening to, for once.

*John exits*

(*Urgently*) We're very late now. (*He glances down at the photos, then throws them on the desk*)

**Rex** (*looking at the photos*) What were you looking for?

**Leonard** (*sharply*) Nothing. I wasn't looking for anything. (*With a slight smile*) What am I going to make them do next, then?

**Rex** (*astonished*) *I* don't know. (*Excitedly, smiling*) It could be so many things. It's got to be something they can photograph for Saturday's front page.

**Leonard** Christ! Look at you, grinning all over your face. You're as bad as Johnson and all the rest upstairs—not that they ever are upstairs. Given half the chance, they'd have the kids tunnelling under the motorway, or buying eighty Leicester Sound "T" shirts each, before being allowed to win.

**Rex** Yes—they will do absolutely anything, those kids. They're desperate just to get into the Studio and meet you, and then the Yellow Jacks and everything as well!! The last concert the Yellow Jacks did here a

girl asked Ross, begged him, to sign her lip. I saw it, and he did and
I wondered if she was going to cut that bit off and keep it in a jam-jar,
so the signature wouldn't come off.

**Leonard** Stop that—you're not going to talk like that in here—understand! *I don't like it.* (*He switches on the music and goes on to the air: the
end of Herb Alpert*)

**Rex** I'm sorry, Leonard.

**Leonard** (*on the air*) Hello, love. How are you, then? Good. I wish you
could see the sight up here. The Studio is brimming with your answers,
they're hanging everywhere. Rex is just handing me the postcards—
perhaps *your* postcard, enabling you to get through to Stage Two.
Hurry, Rex! Had a hard job sorting them, have you, Rex?

**Rex** (*sharing in a double act*) Yes, Leonard. We've been simply wading
through entries.

**Leonard** Up to your knees, were you?

**Rex** Up to our stomachs in some places, up to our mouths, Leonard . . .

**Leonard** You nearly drowned our Rex, love. Pity you didn't send a few
more. (*He begins to read some cards briskly*) Diane Williams of thirty
Sutton Road, says she'd like to go to Scotland with Peter and climb
mountains with him because he's afraid of heights. Quite a sadist,
aren't you, Diane. Thank you for that. Pam Lawrence of ten Rosendale
Avenue says she'd like to go to London with Ross, because that's what
the real prize is. I like that, a real realist, there. Pam will go far, won't
she. Linda Perry of eighteen Horseley Road says she'd like to go to the
moon with Ross, that's a long way to go, Linda. Because he looks so
like an astronaut, and Nicola Davies of thirty-five Pool's Road; rather
a grubby postcard, isn't it, Nicola. Says she'd like to go to Kenya with
Ken, that's a Nicola-type joke, and go on safari because Ken looks so
good in a suntan and so I'm sure, would you, Nicola. You're through
*all the way* to Stage Two, Nicola Davies. There's the music for Stage
Two now, love, and a list of all those that have qualified. Get your lead
pencil ready . . . (*He plays music*)

**Rex** (*nervously*) What happens if we don't think of something, Leonard?

**Leonard** What indeed, Rex. (*With a slight smile*) Disaster.

**Rex** Perhaps some sort of race . . .

**Leonard** There is of course something staring us in the eyeballs *right at
this moment!* Isn't there?

**Rex** (*staring at the desk*) What?

**Leonard** It isn't original. It's been used in America several times. (*He picks
up the "T" shirt*)

**Rex** (*excitedly*) What is it?

**Leonard** And it's rather cheap, not what they're used to.

**Rex** (*louder*) What is it?

**Leonard** They might just enjoy it. *Just.*

**Rex** What is it, Leonard?

**Leonard** (*swinging round*) And it is—they have to make a portrait dummy
of Ross, or any of the others, *Life Size.*

**Rex** What?

**Leonard** A model, effigy. A dummy of one of the Jacks, out of old clothes, like a guy, stuffed full and life size. That's the idea, Rex.

**Rex** That's—that's pretty good, in fact, it's brilliant. (*Loudly*) It is.

**Leonard** It's not at all. It's not even good, but it'll *just* do.

**Rex** (*quietly*) It's great.

**Leonard** (*by the controls*) Christ—listen to that.

**Rex** What?

**Leonard** You can almost hear all their small ears pressed against the radio waiting for it. The competition of the century. (*He brings up the theme music really loud*)

**Rex** You knew the answer all the time, Leonard, didn't you?

**Leonard** (*on the air*) Rex is coming over with all of Stage Two in his hands.

**Rex** Here it is, Leonard—all of it. (*He hands him nothing*)

**Leonard** Thank you, Rex. (*His tone suddenly becomes personal, almost gentle*) O.K., luv, what we want—what I want you to do, love, is very simple and a little special, for the next stage of our remarkable obstacle race to get to the Yellow Jacks and London Town, where everything is still possible. I want you, love, to make in the next two days, a model of one of the boys—(*laughing*)—one of the great Yellow Jacks, a model of Ross or Dave, or Ken, or Pete. "What do you mean, Leonard, make a model, a dummy, how on earth do I do that, Leonard—that's impossible!" Well, love, what you do, is, you get some old clothes, and paper, and stuff it up him, right up and copy his face from a picture, and use some wool for his hair, or go to a gentleman's hairdresser, or even a ladies'. (*In a gentle voice*) Please could I borrow your shavings? No, seriously, love, don't spend any money on it, and get it to me at Leicester Sound by five o'clock Friday. Do you understand now, O.K., love? And the two who make the most wondrous accurate models will become the finalists, and come up here. That can't be bad. It's not. So do your best, love, and hurry, won't you. Good hunting.

*A blast of music*

(*Very abrasively*) I don't like competitions! (*He brings the music up again*)

*The Lights fade to a Black-out*


SCENE 4

*Nicola's room*

*A radio is playing in the background. Nicola is pulling out a pile of magazines methodically from under the bed and side of the room, and a pile of cans, packets, etc., that she has taken from the Supermarket*

**Susan** I don't want to stick around. Don't know why I should.

**Nicola** You said you would. (*She continues to pull stuff out into the room*)

**Susan** What you doing with all of this?

**Nicola** There's not much time.

**Susan** (*suddenly grabbing a poster from the pile*) Hey! You've got one of these. Who's it of? (*She unfolds an enormous pin-up poster of a star, holds it up and looks at it*) Oh, him! You haven't done it, have you? Don't you know the point? (*She lays it out on the floor*) Got it at shop, did you, off the market—they're from America. Don't you know what to do? You have to wet it. (*She lies down on top of it*) Wet it with anything you've got and rub it all over. Rub.

**Nicola** (*moving over*) Yes. (*She rubs hastily, too*) We haven't got time, really.

**Susan** And the top should sort of peel away. (*She is still lying on top of the poster*) And you see all the hair underneath, and you see *everything*. (*She rubs her hand on the poster*) It's not really his body, it's somebody else's and they cut his head off. (*Loudly*) Come on! (*She rubs frantically*) It's too old! (*Loudly*) It doesn't work! (*She rubs again; loudly*) Why not. I *wanted* it to.

**Nicola** Probably never did work. Come on—I've lost time, now. Hurry!

**Susan** (*lying on the poster*) I took one of these to sex education class, she was new then, Miss Booth, thought she'd be interested. She hit me across the face! (*Indicating*) Right there! Girls shouldn't have such things and all that. Why not? I saw her flushing it down the toilet, she talked like a dalek, anyway. I couldn't hear any of her sex education lessons, the traffic noise right by me. (*Loudly*) I never heard any*thing* at school.

**Leonard's Voice** (*on the radio*) That was . . . How are you doing, then? Yes, I mean *you*, whoever you are, wherever you are, you with the sticking-out ears. That's right, keep it up, you haven't got long.

**Nicola** Yes. (*She speeds up collecting all the objects together and gets ready for the stuffing*)

**Susan** He's hurrying you now.

**Leonard's Voice** (*continuing straight on, on the soundtrack*) Rex's bulky shape is beside me here in the Studio as always. (*With sudden mock surprise*) Hey, he's moving away now, don't leave me, Rex, don't leave me. He's going. How can you do this to me, he's left me. I'm alone and afraid. Raindrops might start falling on my head—(*his tone changes*)—and yours, too.

*Music begins—"Raindrops"*

**Nicola** You know, I think he liked me a bit or something when I rang in. He spoke to me longer than the others, different.

**Susan** He only spoke to you longer than the others because he was waiting for the news to come up.

**Nicola** (*to herself*) Ready now! (*Worried*) I'm running out of time, come on! (*She suddenly pulls out the dummy from under the bed, all in pieces, the huge torso, the decapitated head, the hands, the feet, the arms, etc.*)

**Susan** Look at it! You'll never finish that in time.

**Nicola** Got to. Got to fill it up, make it stiff.

**Susan** (*picking up some Supermarket objects*) What are these?

**Nicola** Things I've taken from the shop, things I've nicked. They're all going inside. No use to me. I'm sending them all in this.

**Susan** (*picking up a pot of paint*) How did you get all this paint?

**Nicola** Saved lunch money.

**Susan** (*startled*) What you been eating?

**Nicola** Haven't. Don't need to. I can go for days without eating if I have to. And I am.

**Susan** You'll starve to death, you will. (*Suddenly she picks up the head and a foot*) Is this Ross?

**Nicola** Yes. He's the easiest to do, his face is very simple.

**Susan** (*suddenly loudly*) He's very big.

**Nicola** Yes, I made him big, so he'd notice it.

**Susan** We can do anything we want with him, now all his bits are here. We can stand on his face. (*She stands on it*) Can't we? Pull his tongue out. (*She picks up the torso*) Pull his knickers off . . .

**Nicola** (*loudly*) Don't do that, Susan. You'll tear him—it'll tear.

**Susan** Yes! (*Firmly*) You're really stupid, Nicola. Do you know that even if you get this ready and Leonard just happens to pick it out, which he won't, even then you haven't really started, he can go on forever with you if he likes, *on* and *on* and *on*.

**Nicola** (*determined*) I know that . . .

**Leonard's Voice** (*suddenly piping up*) Hello, how are you doing? Yes, I mean *you*, yes you, with the popping eyes and sticking-out ears.

*They both suddenly stop and stare at the radio. As Leonard's voice continues, Susan picks it up and turns the volume down. Then she sings loudly above it*

I hope I'm not interrupting *you*, am I, because a lady wrote to me to say she had the radio on when, lucky lady, she was giving birth to a baby son, Dominic, and the first sound Baby Dominic heard on this earth was yours truly's ugly, grating tones pouring out. I'm getting worse and worse, aren't I? Stop polluting British steam radio. Great belches of grey filth pouring out of my mouth, straight at you down there. In a moment I'll be talking to John Robinson, who's just come out of the army and Northern Ireland and all the old troubles, and he's come home to talk to me.

**Susan** Hear him. (*She holds the radio up with Leonard's voice pouring out of it*) That's the nearest you'll get to Leonard—this! Not any nearer than that! (*She puts down the radio next to Nicola, having turned the volume up*)

**Leonard's Voice** And now *you*, *you* down there who have entered the competition of the century, time is running out. Here's some music for you.

*Music begins*

**Nicola** Yes! Quick. (*She quickens the stuffing of the dummy with the Supermarket objects*) You're going to help now.

**Susan** No, I don't think I want to, now.
**Nicola** (*swinging round*) *You've got to!*

*Pause*

**Susan** (*loudly*) Why?
**Nicola** Because I'm going to get there. Into the building and see him.
**Susan** (*quietly*) You won't . . .
**Nicola** Come on, there's no time at all now. Paint that yellow, quick!
**Susan** If I have to . . . (*She takes a big brush and splashes huge dollops of yellow paint on the body*)

*Nicola stuffs the legs*

Your room's too small, it'll stink of paint for ever more. You won't be able to live in here any more.
**Nicola** Good. I want that. Hurry—paint.
**Susan** (*sploshing bright yellow paint on the torso: her paint strokes getting faster and faster*) When they played at Coventry, Ken had a blue belt, the others had yellow as usual. I don't like this colour, sort of sick-looking. They ought to change it. You know I had to get back after the concert—it was twelve or after in the night.
**Nicola** (*to herself*) Come on . . . (*She stuffs the legs and head*)
**Susan** I didn't think I could get back. It was raining really hard, straight in your eyes. I got on to the road, started hitching—all these huge lorries went past, enormous. Looked much bigger in the dark. And you know, they all had their radios on. Yes! I could hear. It was Leonard Brazil. It was. He was coming from every single lorry. But none of them stopped.
**Nicola** (*quietly, determinedly*) Come on, quick!
**Susan** (*painting fast*) So I *stood straight* in front of one of them and waved, and he *had* to stop, or flatten me, and he stopped all right, and he opened his door, all smiling and everything, and I got in, and you know what, the seat next to him was still warm, it was all covered with chocolate. Somebody had been sitting there just a moment before—*a girl*.
**Nicola** (*to herself*) Faster.
**Susan** I knew he was going to try to kill me then, yes, on the motorway, in the dark, on the side, where nobody could see, you know, get me on my back and jam a stick of lipstick down my throat, and I'd hear Leonard Brazil on the radio, and suddenly it'd stop, and I'd be dead, and they'd find me in pieces like this—(*indicating the dummy as she paints*)—in a bundle, in the mud, been assaulted, flies in my eyes, and all that. And pictures of me on the telly, me being lifted up and wrapped in a sheet, you know. (*Lightly*) But nothing did happen. Nothing at all. (*Pause. She stops painting. Lightly*) I want it to.
**Nicola** (*suddenly very loudly*) Oh! Look, Susan, it's still not nearly full. (*She stares at the legs and then into the torso*) We've got to fill it up now. (*Very agitatedly*) Now!
**Susan** Put this in, anyway. (*She crumples the huge centrefold picture of the pop-star. As she does so, they both suddenly look up with a jolt and stare at all the posters and ornaments in the room*)

*The same idea hits them both*

**Nicola** (*loudly*) Yes! Come on. Everything . . .

*They suddenly tear down all the posters and ornaments—everything in the room and throw it into the stomach of Ross. The action begins swiftly and ends furiously. It lasts under a minute*

(*As they do it*) Come on down.

**Susan** (*joyfully*) Yes. It's coming down. What's that poster? Come on. (*She rips a poster down*)

*Nicola takes everything off the chest of drawers, all her furry ornaments—everything*

**Nicola** He's got to *be* full.
**Susan** (*loudly*) Yes.

*Susan's pent-up violence comes out in her attack on the posters, whereas Nicola is more methodical, but also very fast. The music on the radio ends*

**Leonard's Voice** (*his tone is very personal*) Hello, there, how's it going, then . . .? Yes, *you*. You down there. Keeping at it, are you, *love*, that's good. (*He brings up music, or a commercial*)
**Nicola** (*throwing in objects*) Go on—in—in—in . . .
**Susan** Come on down. (*She pulls the lightshade off and throws it in*)

*They are both exhausted. The outburst ends, the torso is full. They both stare at it*

**Nicola** It's finished.

*The Lights fade to a Black-out*


SCENE 5

*The Studio. Night*

*A phone-in programme is in progress, the voice of the caller, Jim, about forty, is heard on the telephone, coming out of the monitor speakers. The telephone receiver is off, lying on the desk. Leonard is standing some distance away, at the back of the Studio, smiling and listening. Rex is in his box*

**Jim** (*his voice is heard in the Black-out first*) . . . I mean, don't you agree with me, Leonard, about these vandals, hooligans, whatever you like to call them, I mean, everywhere I go I actually *see* things being smashed up, I see them doing it, and writing things up. I mean, I saw some young thugs—I don't want to use abusive terms, especially on your programme, Leonard, and I certainly won't do so, but these men—they weren't just boys, they were grown men, and they were standing round this flower bed of red tulips, and they pulled up every single one, they were pulling them out, by the roots, tearing them up and treading them into the ground—the whole lot——

*Leonard flicks the switch to cut off the caller in mid-sentence. Silence. He
smiles*

**Leonard** Why do they ring me. Explain me that. Why don't they phone
each other? (*He flicks the switch on again*)

**Jim** —and even more. And apart from that, I don't know if you find this,
I mean as an important person, and obviously on the air—but I mean—
these filthy phone calls—filthy phone calls—people ringing me up——

**Leonard** (*turning the volume down and speaking to Rex through the intercom*) Is he going to start being rude—I think he is. Thank God I only
have to do this twice a week . . . (*He turns the volume up*)

**Jim** —you see what I mean, I don't want to mention anything filthy over
the air of course——

*Leonard holds his finger ready to press the cut-off button*

—and I'm not going to, but I'm always getting wrong phone calls,
people talking to me about things I don't know *anything about*! You
know the feeling of course, being a famous person, Leonard—somebody
rang me the other day, started talking about my horse, how he wanted
to buy it, get hold of it. I mean, I don't have a horse. Is that clear,
Len? I just don't have one. (*Loudly*) What would I do with a bleeding
horse? (*Suddenly very loudly*) What would I do with a fucking horse in
this fuck——

*Leonard cuts him off*

**Leonard** (*smiling, very calm*) I'd like to say goodnight now, Jim, thanks for
that call, it was a Jim-type call. The time is nine twenty-three on the
L.B. night show on this Competition Friday in Competition Week, so
hold on tight. It's raining up here, raining black buckets just outside,
so let's take a dip into the soft inside of Nostalgia Corner, go back to
the golden days of nineteen sixty-seven when London was alive and
wriggling and bursting at the seams, you remember, don't you? Or
perhaps you don't. We were listening to this—some of us were . . . (*He
puts on a record—"See Emily Play" by the Pink Floyd—turning the
volume down after a few bars. He takes off his headphones*) That's enough.
I don't want any more calls—you've already put through too many. I
hate the smell of the new paint in the corridors.

*Rex enters from the box*

(*Loudly*) And *also* I've decided I'm not going to do my spot tonight.

**Rex** What do you mean? Why not?

**Leonard** I have reasons. Got to cope with Stage Three. (*Loudly*) I'm not
doing it. That's final!

**Rex** Some people tune in specially for it. I mean you *must* do it this week
of all weeks—we've never had so many calls, so many entries—perhaps
you should take a few more calls—if you would—it would . . .

**Leonard** I should, should I? No. (*He gets up and starts searching for
something*) I've never liked them—has anyone ever shown you this?

The secret of phone-ins! Where is it—this . . . (*He starts pulling something out of a cupboard*) When we started a colleague made these . . . (*Loudly*) Come on out! (*He pulls really hard. A huge mass of tapes, tangled, without their spools, in an enormous ball, comes out of the cupboard*) Tapes. (*He pulls more out*) Of the phone-ins, hundreds of them—see? (*He holds them up—a vast amount*) There are a lot more all around us, cupboards full, we should tie ourselves up in it, miles and miles of complaints and shouts and whimpers. (*Holding a piece of tape tight*) And FRUSTRATION! (*He runs a finger down the tape*) You half expect to get scalded by them. He edited them, of course, to make them even more comical, more juicy—this disc jockey did.

**Rex** (*smiling*) Great. I must listen to them sometime.

**Leonard** The usual Rex response. Take the whole lot—(*he tosses the mass of tapes at him*)—they can become your bedtime listening, can't they.

**Rex** (*taking an armful of tapes*) There . . .

*A pause. Leonard suddenly stares at Rex*

**Leonard** You realize we're almost alone in this building, we're surrounded by empty corridors. You and me. That's a terrifying thought. I usually have my rest from you at this time.

**Rex** I know. I asked to do extra time specially.

**Leonard** Did you. (*Staring at him*) You know, you're the most ambitious thing on three legs I've ever seen.

**Rex** That's not true. I only want to hang on to my job, don't I? I only want to become good at it.

**Leonard** Only that? I don't believe it.

**Rex** And I enjoy working on your show, of course.

**Leonard** Don't try to tell me that's the only reason for this fantastic obsessional attempt at efficiency.

**Rex** Yes, of course.

**Leonard** (*smiling*) No it's not.

**Rex** (*quietly*) Of course, eventually I want to get on—that's natural, isn't it? (*Smiling*) I want my voice up in lights, eventually.

**Leonard** (*quietly*) That's very good, Rex—for you.

**Rex** (*unblinking*) It's your expression.

**Leonard** (*surprised*) Is it?

**Rex** I heard it over the air, before I was working here. I *still* listen to you all the time. I even sit and listen to you at home, on my days off, when you're on.

**Leonard** (*astonished*) You don't really do that, do you?

**Rex** Yes. (*Smiling lightly*) There's nothing you've said that I don't remember, nothing! I've noticed everything that you've used up here. (*Smiling*) I'm sort of photostating you really—all the time.

**Leonard** (*with a slight smile*) So that's what you're doing. I wish you'd stop it. (*Moving away from him*) You know what you are, Rex, you're reptilian.

**Rex** Yes.

**Leonard** Don't you ever let yourself go—go for a night on the town?

**Rex** No. Neither do you. Do you?

**Leonard** You ought to get yourself another job—I mean that—and quick.

**Rex** Why should I? This is better than anything else I could be doing. I'd be out of work if I was down there. I want to be different, not a crime, is it? And after all, you're good, aren't you? You are. In fact, Leonard, you could actually be the greatest, the best D.J. there's ever been. Couldn't you? Yes, I mean singers become famous one day and are gone the next, but D.J.s go on and on. You will, Leonard—I wonder what the people from Capitol are thinking. You must have got it.

**Leonard** (*loudly*) I told you not to. (*He flicks a switch*) Nine twenty-six on the L.B. night show in Competition Week. We all had a great time at the open-air concert last week, didn't we—it was a true festival, a celebration if ever there was one—the greatest. But I've been asked to point out by the little man in blue—we did leave rather a mess, didn't we? It was six feet high in some places; the farmer couldn't find his sheep, or his own bullocks—they were totally smothered, and he had a job locating his lady wife, found her under a pile of toilet paper and cigarette ends. Seriously, friends, let's try to be cleaner next time, it'll save a lot of hassle. It's black and soaking wet out now, pelting towards us. Next the results of Stage Two—stand by, love, this is it, now, after something from the summer of 'sixty-seven when those topless young things with shining kneecaps bounced down the hot streets of our glorious London. Yeh, that's right.

*Music—"Whiter Shade of Pale" by Procol Harum*

Come on. Bring them in. We'd better get this over.

**Rex** Yes. (*He does not move*) You're playing a lot of oldies tonight.

**Leonard** Yes. (*Abrasively*) I'm in a sentimental mood, aren't I? You're much too young to remember, of course.

**Rex** (*smiling, looking innocent*) Too young to remember what, Leonard?

**Leonard** What do you think? (*Abrasively*) Remember before the rot set in. I'm not in any way nostalgic about that time.

**Rex** (*smiling, watching him*) Oh no?

**Leonard** No I'm not. I'm certainly not one of those mooning leftovers wallowing backwards all the time.

**Rex** No. Of course not.

**Leonard** I know exactly what it was like. (*Loudly*) Exactly!

**Rex** Yes.

**Leonard** (*staring straight at him*) But it's undeniable, Rex, that the music we were producing on that label, seven or eight years ago, was *alive*. That is incontestable. It had gut, it was felt, and it kicked, sometimes savagely. (*Smiling, with more flip*) Because, of course, everything seemed possible. (*Pause*) I was even quite militant in a quiet way. We thought things were changing and all that romantic crap.

**Rex** (*smiling*) Of course you did.

**Leonard** Don't stand there with that idiotic grin on your face!

*Rex does not move*

**Rex** No.
**Leonard** You'd better get on with it, hadn't you, before I decide to take revenge.

*Rex exits*

*Leonard talks to Rex while the latter is off*

You should have been at the open-air concert at the weekend. *It was vile!* It was a perfect example. (*Smiling, slightly mocking*) A grey, shabby echo of the time when festivals really were celebrations. Everybody was lying about in lifeless heaps, mumbling apologetically, and getting bitten by horseflies. You felt you could have turned them over with your foot, and they wouldn't have been able to get up. I saw one girl, a large girl, with a very big face, she wasn't very young, wandering through a patch of long grass. Her face and also her lips were sort of swollen, and completely ashen, almost blue, in fact, as if she was actually physically dead. I almost wanted to go up and touch her; I felt that if you touched that face it would probably flake into nothing. (*Smiling*) In fact I haven't got that picture out of my mind yet.

*Leonard puts on a record of "Baby Face". The music is very loud*

*Rex enters with a barrowload of twenty-five dummies, piled in a huge heap*

**Rex** You've got to make the final choice. (*He lays them on the floor*)
**Leonard** I don't believe it. (*Pause*) I just don't believe it!
**Rex** (*smiling, unconcerned*) What's the matter?
**Leonard** You mean they did it—they actually made them?
**Rex** Yes, of course.
**Leonard** Dressed and everything?
**Rex** You didn't expect them to give us nude models, did you? Though they would have if you'd told them to.
**Leonard** (*picking one up*) We could be in Los Angeles, couldn't we— except it's even worse. Christ, look, they've even painted fingernails on them, bound to be toenails under that. (*He pulls at the shoes; then at the hair*) Probably their own new clothes, too—or their little brother's. They must have worked all through the night on these obscenities. They're burrowing like moles to get up here! Why do they do it—tell me, why?
**Rex** Because you told them to do it.
**Leonard** You could drop anything over the air into that pool and they'd gobble it up. (*Feeling one of the dummies*) What have they got inside them—feel this—feels as if it's stuffed with cans, and packets of frozen food! And all their magazines—clogged with them! How many of these ghastly objects are there?
**Rex** Twenty-eight. Two of them by people we'd eliminated at Stage One, but they still went and made them.

**Leonard** (*picking up another*) This is rapidly becoming a madhouse. We're being invaded by all these. Are they all here?

**Rex** All the best ones. I put some in the canteen—they're propped up in chairs—as a joke when people come in tomorrow.

**Leonard** As a joke? (*He looks at the labels on the dummies, looking for Nicola's*)

**Rex** (*with an innocent smile*) Nothing wrong with that is there? I've put two in the ladies' toilet as well, sitting on the pan. So which two are you going to have—these are the best. Don't mind the paint on this one, it got into its hair as I was pulling it along the corridor.

**Leonard** What?

**Rex** Which two are you going to choose . . .?

**Leonard** These two'll do.

**Rex** (*looking at some cards*) Louise Prentiss and Jane Harris.

**Leonard** All right, get hold of them quickly, get this dealt with and . . . (*Suddenly he looks up*) Whose is that one?

**Rex** (*looking at the cards*) Nicola Davies.

**Leonard** Really—Nicola Davies. I thought so. Well, let's have her instead, shall we? Scrub that one.

**Rex** Why—you chose the other one.

**Leonard** Do as you're told.

**Rex** (*after a pause*) Have you got a thing about her, or something?

**Leonard** (*looking up*) No! (*Pause*) I picked her voice out, I've been using it. (*Looking at the dummy*) They look even more like home-made corpses —take them away.

**Rex** They'll make pretty good photos in the paper tomorrow, anyway.

**Leonard** (*looking up*) I don't like that.

**Rex** (*looking up*) What?

**Leonard** I don't like it, do you hear. You ought to have stopped me thinking of it.

**Rex** *I* should have . . .?

**Leonard** (*really working himself up*) What do you think you're paid for? I mean this idea was trash. It was unpleasant, incompetent, lazy— (*throwing down a dummy*)—it's trash!

**Rex** Why?

**Leonard** If you can't see that there's no hope for you!

**Rex** (*smiling*) No hope for me, is there?

**Leonard** I need somebody that's going to think, *think*, don't I?

**Rex** Yes, Leonard, I——

**Leonard** (*interrupting*) Not just a callous, unquestioning, secret police vegetable——

**Rex** (*interrupting*) It isn't my fault . . .

**Leonard** (*carrying on, in a real outburst*) —you'd be one of the first to come and take us away, wouldn't you! *Wouldn't you!* Come here!

**Rex** It was your idea, Leonard.

**Leonard** You're an abortion, really, aren't you—with absolutely no imagination. Nothing! A complete abortion.

**Rex** (*loudly*) I didn't think of it, Leonard, did I—it wasn't me——

**Leonard** (*interrupting*) You're a bloody idiot, aren't you.

**Rex** It wasn't me, Leonard—was it?

**Leonard** Get out of here, go on.

*Rex does not move*

Go on, get out!

*Rex moves away quickly, and goes to his box*

**Leonard** (*shouting*) You're fired. Fired! You really are this time. I don't want to see you in this room again. You leave tomorrow. (*Complete silence for a moment. He faces the record desk and fades out the record*) That was "Baby Face", and *this is* the Competition of the Century. And now we have come to that solemn moment—the finalists—the two people who are going to come all the way up here. Gauleiter Rex has written the two names out in red ink—you all did so well—showed enormous determination—the greatest in England. But the two who got through—the two names on the card are—Jane Harris and Nicola Davies. Jane and Nicola have won through to the Final. (*He puts on a fanfare, then fades it down*)

**Rex** (*quietly, matter-of-factly, over the intercom*) I can only get one of them, Mr Brazil, the other one has gone to bed, she must have been very confident. I've got Nicola Davies for you.

**Leonard** Put her through then, Rex. Hello there, Nicola Davies.

**Nicola's Voice** (*coming over the monitor, quietly*) Yes, hello.

**Leonard** Hello, there, Nicola—I don't know if you've been listening to your radio—but I've rung to tell you, in front of the listening thousands, that you have reached the Final, the final round of Competition of the Century.

*Pause*

**Nicola** (*flat, unsurprised*) Have I . . .? Oh, good.

**Leonard** (*louder*) Did you ever think you could make it, Nicola?

**Nicola** (*matter-of-factly*) No.

**Leonard** Are you tall or short?

**Nicola** Not tall—quite short.

**Leonard** Rex said tall—I said short. You've got a short-type voice. What are you wearing now, love—what is Nicola wearing?

**Nicola** I'm wearing—I'm wearing a belt and top and trousers—and no shoes.

**Leonard** No shoes. (*Pause*) I see. Ross'll like that. I'm looking forward to meeting you, Nicola Davies, tremendously. Aren't you?

**Nicola** Yes, I am. I am, Leonard—(*flatly*)—very much.

**Leonard** Good—that's good. Nicola's going to be coming up here—I'm sure we'll get on. Tomorrow's going to be an extraordinarily good day, isn't it? There'll be some big surprises, I'm sure, and there's a big surprise now—do you usually stay to listen to the L.B. spot?

**Nicola** Oh, yes.

**Leonard** Well, Nicola, I have news for you. You are in it, you are in the

L.B. spot. For each week, for those of you who have never listened before, and if there are any they'll be hung, drawn, and fined—L.B. has his spot, when he unleashes a few things. Are you still there, Nicola?
**Nicola** Yes. I'm here.
**Leonard** Well, you're high up, high up in the L.B. spot—high in the clouds. And the first—the first L.B. moment is, it's my birthday today, so I'm told, which is a lie because it's at least two years until my next birthday, and our friend Rex—who is definitely getting ideas—has made a cake. A cake out of melted-down records. I have in front of me—(*he puts a book in front of himself*)—a pile of records squashed together with a cherry on top, thank you, Rex, that's just the type of cake I deserve. (*Loudly, in a runny voice*) I deserve it—what am I saying? (*In an American accent*) What's gone wrong with him? Seriously, folks, I've been thinking about London, for a number of enormous reasons—London, capital of this fine country of ours. And of course it's the prize in the Competition of the Century. (*Quickly*) I was walking along Carnaby Street the other day, Nicola, it shows how old I am, I can pronounce that name correctly, yes I was there—I was Lord Kitchener's grand-daughter—the street that made the world swing—you should see what it looks like now—it looks like a museum street, it needs its glass case—especially as half of it has been knocked down. The Americans, I hear, are going to ship it off soon across the seas—it'll be our last export, our swinging relics. They're shipping it off to Texas to stand in the desert somewhere, where it'll ooze away under the midday sun. We mustn't get bitter! (*In a funny voice*) Your mouth tastes bitter, Brazil, it's going black round the edges. Remember where you are. You can't let the side down like this, Brazil. It's an important moment. Brazil, what are you doing? (*Quieter*) What does he think he's doing? No—seriously, everybody, London's still an exciting place—the most exciting place. The only place to be. It's still brown and beautiful. Why brown—why not? Mustn't get obsessed by all our yesterdays, they're gone, thank goodness, must get obsessed by all our tomorrows. (*Like a machine*) Hear hear. Hear hear. Hear hear. Don't spit on the animals—I said don't spit on the animals—where's Nicola Davies—where is she? Still there, Nicola?
**Nicola** Yes, Leonard, I'm still here.
**Leonard** (*smiling*) The rain is slashing at the windows. I'm afraid, Nicola, if it gets to me I may melt. I'm afraid. Hear that, Nicola?
**Nicola** Yes. I heard.
**Leonard** No need to fear, Nicola is here. I have a note here, what do D.J.s really do while they're playing records? That's a good question. I hate to tell you. Some read the papers, some play the stockmarket, call up their stockbrokers between records—that's true, folks—some call up their lady friends, and some just play with their stylus. (*Smiling*) And some long to scream obscenities over the air! The mad D.J. And they all use words so sumptuously for your pleasure. Do you ever listen to your words, Brazil? Never, thank goodness, but never mind. Everybody needs us, after all—we're the new jokers of the pack, we're the

new clowns, we tell it how it should be. And we're going to lick the blues. Each week I try to lick the blues—this time with a fly-sprayer, I have it out, I'm spraying it, I'm spraying them now, they're falling to the ground, curling up black and dead, legs in the air—we've done it. Don't spit on the animals. We're going to make it, aren't we, get through to the other side, of course we are—and if you've just seen some horrible things, on the television, bomb blasts, unemployment, politicians, and all that part of our good old England, and you've switched it off to listen to me, sensibly! Then remember, no need to fear, we're going to lick it, so Shout it out! Things can only get better and better—so Shout it out! We have the greatest day of the century tomorrow, so there's something to look forward to, so let's Shout it out! Yes, you, madam, get out of the bath and *Shout it out!* And you, love, take your hands away from here and Shout it out! Throw that away, lad, and SHOUT IT OUT! Come on, grandad, SHOUT IT OUT! You too, Nicola Davies, Shout it out! Let's have some real music. I said SHOUT IT OUT! LOUDER!

*Rex comes from his box and stares at Leonard in silence*

I can't hear you, don't spit on the animals—this is nineteen hundred and seventy-six, this is Len Brazil—this is crazy competition week— be there tomorrow—and once more SHOUT IT OUT! (*He brings the music to a crescendo then fades it out*)

*Rex whistles*

Shit! I wasn't going to do that. (*He flicks a switch, the music comes on, loud*)

*The Lights fade to a Black-out*

INTERVAL

*In the Black-out we hear two girls' voices singing "I Can Give You Love",
one of the Yellow Jacks' songs. They sing the whole of the first verse loudly
and slightly harshly to a piano accompaniment, woodenly played. The Lights
come up*

*Nicola's bedroom. Saturday lunchtime*

*Nicola is sitting on the bed, brushing her hair. Susan moves round the room,
munching some cheese puffs. There is a packet with one sandwich on a shelf*

**Susan** You ought to eat something.
**Nicola** I don't need to. Not hungry.
**Susan** (*turning away*) You won't do very well if you don't eat. Here.

*Susan tosses Nicola some cheese puffs. Nicola does not bother to catch
them*

**Nicola** No, don't want anything. (*Smiling*) Good sort of diet, this com-
petition, I lost a lot. See—it's come off. (*She feels her waist*)
**Susan** You don't need to lose any. (*Pause*) You're getting skinny. (*Pause*)
You look a bit pale, you know.
**Nicola** I want to look pale.
**Susan** They coming for you in a car?
**Nicola** No, I'm going there.
**Susan** (*turning round the room*) They can't even be bothered to fetch you.
Not much left in your room, is there. (*Smiling*) All this, has sort of
cleaned it out, hasn't it? I mean the competition . . .
**Nicola** Yes, I put most of it in, didn't I. It all came in useful.
**Susan** (*to herself*) Anyway, there's the concert tonight. (*Smiling, looking
at her*) Is that the lipstick I bought with you—it made my lips go sore,
and they itched like anything. (*She rubs her lip*) Still itch all the time,
if I think about them. I want to get some white lipstick. I'm growing
old, do you know that? (*She looks at Nicola*) Yes! How do you feel
then—about it?
**Nicola** O.K. Fine. (*Quietly*) I'm going to be all right. I've been preparing
for it. Sat here by the record-player all night, listening to records all
night, really quietly so no-one could hear me.
**Susan** (*very lightly*) It'd be more exciting, wouldn't it really, if you were
going to be shot if you lost, or something like that. I mean, then you
really would be nervous. If they were going to put you in the electric
chair, tie you up in a black chair, and press the button, and—(*smiling*)—

instead they'll just give you a consolation prize if you lose—that's not very exciting, is it? (*Picking up the packet of cheese puffs*) You're very lucky, anyway—you could be going to London. Never been out of this town, have you?

**Nicola** Not really, hardly.

**Susan** And you've already won that L.P. . . . .

**Nicola** They haven't sent it yet.

**Susan** (*excitedly*) Going with them to London, Nicola, you can't do much better than that.

**Nicola** Well I've got into there anyway—into the radio building. (*With a slight smile*) I'm going there.

**Susan** If you go with them—you'll have to be careful of the heavies—they'll still have their heavies with them, they go everywhere with them—when they were playing in Newcastle in March or whenever it was, and I went, you know—and you know what happened, somebody I saw—she was throwing herself down on the carpet the whole time at the exit, after the concert, and when they picked her up, she just threw herself down again, and they got angry, the heavies did, so they kicked her—not that hard—they kicked her, one did, and so anyway, after a bit, she got up, and went and lay down somewhere else—and she made herself sick or something on the floor, in a pool—so this heavy, he wasn't one of the biggest, but he came over to her—and he said something, I couldn't hear it, and she didn't move, so he got her by the hair, not very hard, but he got her by the hair and rubbed her face in it, like that. I saw it. Gave her a quick rub—(*she demonstrates with the head of the teddy-bear by the bed*)—just once—to stop her doing it.

**Nicola** You've told me before. That's not going to happen to me.

**Susan** (*quickly*) I didn't tell you—didn't tell you this. That same time, by the place, I was walking along, and I saw this policeman, he wasn't very old for a policeman, he can't have been that old, he was standing in a doorway, I saw him, he was all by himself and he was swearing his head off, he was, with his teeth kind of clenched. And he had water in his eyes, he was crying, well I don't know if he was really crying but his face was all screwed up and red, and really vicious looking, and there was stuff coming out of his eyes. Down his face. He wasn't old. I saw him anyway, it's true. I remember it more than anything else.

*The phone rings. Nicola answers it*

**Nicola** Yes . . .

**Rex's Voice** (*on the phone; very softly, barely audible*) Nicola Davies?

**Nicola** Yes.

*Pause*

**Leonard's Voice** (*on the phone; very suddenly*) Hallo there, Nicola—this is Leonard here, sorry to drop in like this, we're on the air, love—(*in a funny voice*)—in front of the listening thousands—at this moment. I've just been talking to your fine opponent, Jane, and I wanted to know, love, are you O.K.?

**Susan** What's he ringing you up again for?

**Nicola** (*on the phone*) Yes—I'm very well, thank you.

**Leonard's Voice** Getting a good lunch, are you—what have you had?

**Nicola** For lunch—some water.

**Leonard's Voice** Some water—is that all?

**Nicola** Yes. I'm fine, thank you.

**Leonard's Voice** You must have something else, Nicola, to get really ready for it.

**Nicola** Yes, Leonard.

**Leonard's Voice** The reason I've called, love, is so that we both can tell all the people listening that DON'T FORGET, it's the Competition of the Century today.

**Nicola** Yes.

**Leonard's Voice** And don't you forget that you're having your photographs taken.

**Nicola** No, I won't, Leonard.

**Leonard's Voice** (*after a slight pause*) O.K., love—we'll be seeing each other very soon, so till then, 'bye, love.

**Nicola** (*quietly*) Good-bye. (*She puts down the receiver*)

**Susan** Can't leave you alone, can he?

**Nicola** No—that's good, isn't it? I think he likes me. I'm going to meet him. (*Smiling*) I am.

**Susan** Yes, you really are, aren't you. Leonard Brazil. Do your mum and dad know about this . . .?

**Nicola** They've gone out. I told them—don't think they believed me, or they didn't hear properly—Mum would have listened to the programme —she might have got excited—but they don't like me doing that much.

**Susan** (*hardly listening*) You wearing just that . . .?

**Nicola** Yes.

**Susan** You should put this on. (*She pulls out another dress*) You want to look a bit sexy, don't you—get him excited . . .

**Nicola** This is O.K.

**Susan** He'll probably give you a bit of a squeeze, quick squeeze at your tits.

**Nicola** No he won't—don't be stupid.

**Susan** You know what to do don't you, tell him you're deaf in one ear.

**Nicola** Why?

**Susan** So you can ask for every question to be said twice. Also it'll get him on your side, won't it? You got to try everything you can think of to win. And you'll have to be really on the look-out, won't you— he'll try to put you through a lot for something as big as that—he's not going to give something like that away easily, is he—come on, I'll do that. (*She snatches a hair-brush from Nicola and begins to brush Nicola's hair*) He'll probably hold up pictures of Ross in the nude, to put you off, you ought to put spikes on your shoes—so you can kick him under the table—that's what you've got to do.

**Nicola** (*quietly, determinedly*) I'm going to win, you know.

**Susan** Yes; well if the other one wins we'll really do her, won't we? We'll finish her. (*She moves away*)

**Nicola** (*sharply*) Why don't you ever keep still?

**Susan** Because I don't.

**Nicola** You're always doing that.

**Susan** Why shouldn't I? What's the point of keeping still—I've never kept still. (*Moving up to Nicola*) Come on, you're going to eat something now. (*Picking up a sandwich*) Come on.

*Nicola does not take it*

(*Suddenly very loudly*) Come on, YOU GOT TO EAT! Now open your gob. (*She pushes the sandwich towards Nicola*) I might come to London with you, you know—if you ever get through. Which you probably won't.

**Nicola** (*chewing*) You going to be listening?

**Susan** (*with a slight smile*) I expect so. You ought to stay in London, don't you think—if you get there? We both ought to. Yes. Get out of here! (*She pushes the sandwich into Nicola's mouth*) Come on, eat it all, get it down. Swallow it, Nicola. (*Loudly*) YOU'VE GOT TO! RIGHT DOWN!

*Nicola swallows*

Now you're ready.

*The Lights fade to a Black-out*

SCENE 7

*The Studio*

*John is sitting; Leonard standing; Mick sweeping the floor. Leonard moves around, speaking to Rex, who is not there*

**Leonard** I want these seats adjusted—could I please have these seats adjusted . . .? Where is he? (*Swinging round*) And if that phone rings once more I will have it decapitated. (*Slight pause*) It's that oily sod Johnson, he——

*The phone rings and interrupts Leonard. He picks it up fast. We hear a slimy, nasal voice speaking fast on the other end. We catch a few words*

**Voice** Leonard—a few words' again—congratulations—just want to remind you—Studio A—security . . .

*As he speaks, Leonard's replies are brusque*

**Leonard** (*on the phone*) Yes. . . . Yes. . . . Yes. . . . Quite. . . . Yes. . . . All right. . . . (*Louder*) O.K. . . . Fine! (*He slams the phone down*) Keeps congratulating me on how things are going. That one was to tell me the precise arrangements for Ross's visit to this building—and not to forget to plug the rest of their tour—and remember you're carrying a bumper lot of commercials . . .

**John** (*smiling*) It's going very well, isn't it. I haven't seen anything like this for a long time. I like this atmosphere tremendously.

**Leonard** (*by the coffee machine*) Yes. (*Quietly, looking at the machine*) Do you think if one kicked this machine it'd start playing music?

**John** Is what I hear true?

**Leonard** (*taking coffee from the machine*) What do you hear, John?

**John** That you've been made an offer—that you-know-who have made a whopping big offer . . .

**Leonard** (*matter-of-factly*) Yes. (*Pause*) It appears I have been offered the job . . .

**John** (*smiling*) What? You really have. Congratulations! That's wonderful news, isn't it! (*He smiles*) The station must be really pleased—when you've just started making us a profit.

*Rex enters*

Have you heard? He's been made a firm offer!

**Rex** (*smiling*) He hasn't! Have you, Leonard?

**Leonard** (*matter-of-factly*) Nice, isn't it?

**Mick** Right, err, can I just say, Mr Brazil, how pleased I am that—I mean can I congratulate you—I mean . . . It's really great, isn't it—really great, you'll show them in London . .

**Leonard** Yes, Mick.

**Mick** They won't have seen anything like it, you must be feeling great now, I would be.

**Leonard** That's right, Mick, thank you.

**John** When do you take up residence—after this holiday?

**Leonard** I'm not sure, John, that I'm going at all.

**Rex** What?

**John** What do you mean, you don't know?

**Leonard** We'll be seeing about that.

**John** Well, there's a lot of money there, and the size of the audience— you'll be playing to an audience of millions—you've always been good at that.

**Leonard** (*smiling at him, his manner dangerously light*) That's right—that's very true, John.

*Rex moves around the studio, getting ready*

(*To John, quickly*) I think we should put some music behind you today— don't you? Behind the News. A French horn perhaps, sounding your approach—so you seem to gallop in here on horseback, and a banjo under you for the lighter parts . . .

**John** Don't think we quite need that . . .

**Leonard** You were a good idea of mine, you know, John.

**John** (*with a slight smile*) Of course I was.

**Leonard** My stroke of genius—saying we must have live news and not network.

**John** (*to Rex*) It's the best thing that's ever happened to me—I'd been cut back, one of the many to be lopped off the paper; I was lucky.

**Leonard** (*laughing*) And I've never been able to take the news seriously since. Like most newsreaders, of course, you have no idea what you're saying—when you read it out. Have you?

**John** Of course I do.

**Leonard** (*loudly*) Rubbish! Last week I wrote items of total schoolboy gibberish—announcing that the Third World War had just broken out and was due to arrive in five minutes and that the entire Royal family had contracted rabies—and I asked the girl downstairs—Carol—to slip them in. You came in here, sat down, and read them straight out without a blink. (*He grins*) Without any comment. (*In an American accent*) You're highly dangerous, John.

**John** (*startled*) You didn't do that . . . ? When was that? (*He realizes*) You had me for a moment. (*He smiles; to Rex*) He can take in anybody really if he wants to. (*Smiling*) This man's rather good, you know—he's rather good.

**Rex** Yes, of course. (*He collects a tray covered in letters and small parcels wrapped in coloured paper*) Here's two letters for you. (*He drops them in front of Leonard*) And all these presents and good-luck cards have come in for the two girls. They've been pouring in all the time before they were even chosen. Some are from old age pensioners, shows how wide our audience is, and some are really aggressive and jealous ones from other kids.

**Leonard** (*glancing briefly at his own letters*) Make sure they get one letter each—a pleasant one, Rex. And get this place tidy—we're going to have guests.

**Rex** (*not moving*) Look at that, he hardly glances at his letters. His mother could have died for all we know, or his lady friends could have started eating each other—(*to John*)—a different one each week—and he'd never show anything.

**Leonard** (*putting the letters away*) Yes.

**Rex** And have you heard about his flat? It is totally bare, almost, except for hundreds of books.

**John** Yes, I know.

**Rex** And you know he's hardly eaten all week—so I hear. Gone off his food.

**John** The nervous strain—with this offer hanging over him. (*Smiling*) I hope you're going to give us a great show, Leonard—for all the family.

**Rex** Of course he is.

**John** It's a specially cold day, freezing, out there. Wonderful, isn't it? Everybody'll be indoors, you've got them sitting there already. Probably going to get the biggest audiences we've ever had.

**Leonard** (*looking up*) Well, Rex is not going on the air today, is he? He's not going near a microphone.

**Rex** What?

**Leonard** (*lightly*) He's having no part of this competition.

**Rex** (*startled*) What do you mean by that? (*Getting excited*) What on earth . . .

**Leonard** You're not going on the air, that's what I mean. You've been fired.

**Rex** What? You didn't mean that, did you? But I've been working things out for it . . . What do you mean? (*Working himself up*) I've worked all week on this competition—I have, haven't I?

**Leonard** (*matter-of-factly*) I think you'd better leave us alone, John, the boy's getting excited. Go on, go and find some really juicy news. (*With a slight smile*) Must have something good, mustn't we?

**John** (*getting up*) And what if there isn't any?

**Leonard** Use your imagination, of course. Write some.

*John exits*

**Rex** (*as soon as John exits*) What do you mean I can't do anything?

**Leonard** You can't—I've decided.

**Rex** But I must, don't you see—I . . .

**Leonard** (*dryly*) No. It's not good for you, is it?

**Rex** What do you mean it's not good for me? (*Loudly*) Why have you decided to do this?

**Leonard** I've told you.

**Rex** I mean when everything was going so well for you. (*Loudly*) Why?

**Leonard** I don't think you should be let loose, Rex. So I fired you.

**Rex** You don't really mean that, do you? Do you?

*Leonard does not reply*

(*He changes his tone*) Look, please, Leonard, please, I've prepared something specially. I have. Just for today please. I've been waiting all week for this. (*Loudly*) I am asking you, Leonard. I've worked well for you, haven't I? HAVEN'T I?

**Leonard** (*smiling*) You're not going on the air, Rex, and that's final. You're going to run things more efficiently than you've ever done—for the last time. And you're not going to make a single mistake. Go on.

**Rex** No. (*He does not move*)

*Leonard looks up*

I've got to do something.

**Leonard** (*looking at him*) Why have you got to?

**Rex** Because I want to. (*Matter-of-factly*) Because I'm determined.

**Leonard** You're determined, are you?

**Rex** Yes, Leonard.

**Leonard** (*matter-of-factly*) You worry me, you know, Rex.

**Rex** (*quietly*) Do I?

**Leonard** You can have just one minute. Sixty seconds. I shouldn't let you, of course—you're still fired. You're leaving after the competition.

**Rex** Thanks. Thank you, Leonard.
**Leonard** I should keep your thanks till afterwards. You've got a job to do, do it.

*Rex moves off*

You know this equipment is about to expire, don't you. When it gets hot, it smells really tired—probably give out today.
**Rex** (*smiling happily*) It'll last. It doesn't matter what it looks like.

*Rex exits*

**Leonard** One wouldn't want to do an operation with rusty instruments, would one? (*Looking at the equipment*) This is all really tawdry.

*Rex re-enters quickly*

**Rex** There's one of them out there.
**Leonard** One of them?
**Rex** One of the girls.
**Leonard** Well, bring her in, of course. Don't let her wait out there.

*Rex exits*

(*Matter-of-factly*) Better see what we've netted, hadn't we.

*Rex enters with Nicola*

**Rex** Here.
**Leonard** Hello. (*Pause*) Which one are you?
**Rex** Nicola.
**Leonard** (*gently*) Let her speak for herself.
**Nicola** Nicola Davies.
**Leonard** Nicola Davies. (*Pause*) I thought you'd look a little different . . .
**Nicola** (*embarrassed*) Oh. Did you?
**Leonard** Do I look different?
**Nicola** No—not really.
**Leonard** So you're in the studio now. (*To Rex*) Have they checked her downstairs?
**Rex** I don't think so—she just wandered in—after they'd done the photo outside.
**Leonard** You'd better do it. (*To Nicola, gently*) I'm afraid it's ridiculous, but everybody that comes up here has to be submitted, that's what they call it, to a bomb-check. I'm sorry—it ought to have been downstairs.
**Nicola** Oh—yes. I didn't know. (*She opens her bag*)

*Rex looks through it*

**Leonard** Rex'll do the honours.

*As Rex is searching her*

We get hoaxes all the time—twice as much at night. Last week somebody phoned in to say there was a purple bomb, whatever that meant. (*To Rex*) That's O.K. Thank you. (*Smiling at Nicola*) You like to sit down— careful where you sit. Do you want something to eat? We'll try to get you anything you like.

*Rex goes into the box*

**Nicola** No, thank you. (*She sits to one side*)
**Leonard** We're nearly ready for you. (*He puts his headphones on. To Rex in the box*) O.K., stand by. Where's the other one? (*He presses a button*)

*There is a roar of music, really loud: "The Man Who Sold the World". Nicola starts. Leonard fades the music down*

Don't worry, nothing in the world to worry about. (*He fades the music down. The red light comes on. Into the mike*) Stop where you are! Don't switch off! For I, L.B., am here. This is Crazy Competition Week. This is the final programme—how are you all? On this savage, cold day . . . it's warm up here, though. So this is the Big One. For me, too. We've all got to it, and we're going straight into it, folks. (*In a funny voice*) Get the bleeder over and wrapped up. Both girls are smiling, just a little bit tense; we'll be meeting them in a moment. Right now, let's hear one of the prizes in full flow—and he'll lead us into a few bubbling commercials . . .

**Ross's Voice** (*on tape*) The things I don't like—that's a difficult one. I like most things.
**Leonard** (*cutting off the tape, looking at Nicola*) Know that voice?
**Nicola** Yes—it's Ross's voice.
**Leonard** Rex—we're minus one girl. (*He smiles and flicks a switch*)
**Ross's Voice** I don't like violence—of any sort, of course, or people that provoke it, create it, you know, exploit it, they're criminals really, aren't they?
**Leonard** (*switching it off*) He's in fine form, isn't he?
**Nicola** Yes.
**Leonard** (*calmly, smiling*) They're waiting for the Competition of the Century down there—(*looking at Nicola*)—and we may not be able to give it to them. (*He flicks the switch on again*)
**Ross's Voice** I mean *we* don't use violence—I know people, some morons and journalists, have said so, but everybody just has a party when we play.
**Leonard** Got a good voice, hasn't he?
**Nicola** Yes.
**Ross's Voice** (*in the background, as Nicola and Leonard talk*) And I don't like parasites, journalists, reporters, people that criticize.
**Leonard** (*calmly, smiling*) Rex—come here.

*Rex immediately comes down from the box*

**Ross's Voice** (*as Rex comes down*) And write malicious things about people —and also I don't like people that get above themselves.

*Leonard switches him off*

**Leonard** I was thinking, we'd better give them something to drink, something a little strong, so they don't worry.

**Rex** That's a good idea.

**Leonard** Go and arrange it.

*Rex moves. Leonard is still very calm*

And you'd better find the other one, hadn't you, wherever she is, we need her in one minute . . .

**Rex** (*smiling*) Right, Leonard.

*Rex exits*

**Leonard** (*to Nicola*) You O.K.?

**Nicola** (*quiet*) Yes.

*Leonard flicks the switch again*

**Ross's Voice** I'm not a prude—Christ, you've only got to ask Ken or Dave, or any of my friends, but I really don't like sex where it doesn't belong, I mean . . .

*Leonard switches it off*

**Leonard** (*matter-of-factly*) You better come and sit over here, love, please. Plenty of time, there's nothing to worry about.

*Nicola moves over to a chair by the microphone*

Looking forward to it? (*Pause*) Are you?

**Nicola** Yes—I am.

**Leonard** Good. Don't suppose you ever thought you'd be here.

**Nicola** No—I sort of hoped . . .

**Leonard** And you are. You're here. (*Quietly*) This is the big one, Nicola. You want to listen to him, do you? (*He flicks on a switch as he settles Nicola into a chair, adjusts its height and tests the distance from the microphone*) Are you comfortable?

*Nicola nods; as this happens, Ross's voice booms loudly from speakers in the background*

**Ross's Voice** I mean I agree with that too, and I don't like women who swear. I like them to be—I know this is corny—I like them to be feminine, I'm afraid so, and—I know this list's getting kind of long, I'm in fact a very tolerant person, but you know one thing I really don't like is dirty cutlery. I mean it happens in England, it's much better in the States, but you book in to a really good hotel, and you wake up in the morning for your breakfast, and the first thing you see is dirty cutlery, really filthy cutlery, I mean people don't work in this country, I mean that's the trouble really, isn't it, and somebody really has got to do something—I like cheerful music.

*Rex enters*

*Leonard switches Ross off*

**Rex** She's here.

*Jane enters*

And she's been checked.

*Rex exits*

**Leonard** Hello, I'm Leonard—cut it fine, didn't you?
**Jane** I'm sorry. I couldn't find it. I am sorry—it's not easy to find.

*Rex enters with a tray with wine, glasses and two roses*

**Leonard** It's O.K., love, you're here now. We're ready to go. (*To Rex*)
Have you got the drink?
**Rex** Yes, I have. (*He produces a bottle and moves to get the glasses*)
**Leonard** (*to Jane*) Come and sit here—do you want a drink?
**Jane** I don't know.
**Leonard** (*pouring some out*) Come on, have some, it won't bite you.

*Nicola drinks*

**Rex** Jane doesn't want any.
**Leonard** (*jocularly*) Don't know why we don't give them vitamin injec-
tions as well. Nothing to worry about, girls, I'm just going to ask you
a few questions, don't worry about anything I might do, I'm not going
to sit here, I may roam about . . .
**Rex** (*at the tray—on the side*) I thought they'd like a rose each—a present
from Leicester Sound—two white roses, make them look nice . . .
**Leonard** (*lightly*) They look nice anyway—don't you. Do you want to
wear them? Rex's little gift.

*Jane nods, Rex pins a rose on her; Leonard hands a rose to Nicola*

(*To Rex, referring to Jane*) She needs to be a little higher.
**Rex** Yes. That was a low-key start. (*He goes to the box*)
**Leonard** Of course—this is a family show. (*He puts on his earphones*) O.K.,
that's enough, stop fiddling with her. (*To the girls, smiling*) Now don't
worry, nobody's going to get hurt, are they? (*He flicks a switch*) Before
the commercials that was the one and only Ross, who'll be entering this
building very soon. We have the two lucky and lovely girls with me.
Hello, Nicola.
**Nicola** Hello.
**Leonard** And now Jane—who's looking very composed. Rex has just
given them a couple of roses—one of course white, the other is red—
we have a real War of the Roses coming up here. I wish you could
smell them, breathe into the mikes, girls.

*Jane leans forward, he restrains her*

Here come the questions, glistening on a silver tray. (*He picks up some white cards from the desk*) Thank you, Rex.

**Rex** (*loudly, excitedly, importantly*) We've got one of the biggest audiences we've ever had—it's a great sight. The studio's looking very fine. The competitors are in perfect condition, sleek and healthy, and there's traffic jams for miles . . .

**Leonard** Enough of this gibber! You're going to make some noises, aren't you?

**Rex** I am indeed, Leonard—I'm going to make this noise for a right answer. (*He presses a loud bell*)

**Leonard** That's a nice noise for a right answer.

**Rex** And this noise for a wrong answer. (*He makes a loud vicious buzzing noise*)

**Leonard** That's a grisly noise for a wrong answer.

**Rex** And I'll be making this noise for "Don't knows". (*He makes a funny, irritating noise*)

**Leonard** Yes, girls—*no* "don't knows"—have a guess. If you say "don't know"——

*Rex makes the noise*

—you lose a life; if you lose three lives, you're out of the game, and if it's a tie——

**Rex** If it's a tie . . .

**Leonard** (*quietly*) —we want *you* to vote, ladies and gentlemen, for who put up the best show—so keep your ears skinned, or peeled, or however you like your ears done.

**Rex** Where are the other questions, Leonard?

**Leonard** In my head, Rex.

**Rex** And——

**Leonard** (*cutting Rex off suddenly*) And this now—this here—is—the Competition of the Century. (*Quietly, matter-of-factly*) Jane and Nicola are the contestants. I, Len Brazil, am putting the questions. (*Quietly*) Five, four, three, two, one, ZERO! And the very first question is for Jane. And the question is: Jane—(*quickly*)—how old is Ken?

**Jane** Ken? He's—twenty-one.

*Rex's bell rings loudly*

**Leonard** Correct! The lady is correct. Do you know how many months?

**Nicola** (*quickly*) Six.

**Leonard** It's Jane's question, Nicola.

**Jane** Six months.

*The bell rings again*

**Leonard** One point to Jane. (*Suddenly loudly*) Jane has one point! (*His manner begins to quicken. He has the D.J. instinct coming out despite himself*) And the first question for Nicola is—the question in Round

One for Nicola is, and she's looking very calm—is: what is Dave's favourite food—and when does he like to eat it?

**Nicola** Dave's favourite food—it's fresh—it's home-made bread, and he likes it in the morning. (*Silence. Nervously*) At sunrise, I think.

*The Bell rings loudly*

**Leonard** That's correct, Nicola. (*Rising, moving around past his mike*) That's the answer that was wanted. You're doing fine, Nicola. So is Jane, both of you are doing fine. Round Two of the Competition of the Century. Another Nicola question. Tell me, Nicola, which famous historical and Shakespearean character is traditionally associated with Leicester?

**Nicola** What? (*Pause*) I . . .

**Leonard** A famous character by Will Shakespeare, associated with this fine city of ours. Have to hurry you . . .

**Nicola** I'm sorry—I—I don't know.

*Rex makes a very loud buzz*

**Leonard** You mustn't say that, Nicola, I'm afraid . . . it's not allowed. So you have to lose a life, don't you. Nicola has lost a life. Do *you* know, Jane?

**Jane** (*about to reply, then deciding not to*) I—I—(*she shakes her head*)—I don't . . .

**Leonard** Careful. No "don't knows". Neither of the girls know. Which is a surprise! The answer is King Lear—the man with the long beard. (*He moves, picks up the next question, loudly*) And now, Jane, what is the name of the new office block near the prison?

**Jane** That—it's called—I think it's called the New Walk Centre.

*The bell rings*

**Leonard** Correct. She has given a right answer. Well up on this fine city of ours, aren't you. Good. (*In a funny voice*) It's completely changed since I was a lad here. It's been torn up and replanted. You've got two points now, Jane. You're doing well. You're both doing well. Here's another question for you, Nicola Davies—wait for it—when was the Haymarket Centre opened?—Nicola—the great Haymarket Centre. What was the year when its full glory was seen?

**Nicola** I—I . . . (*She bites her lip*) Was it about ten years ago?

*Rex gives the loud "Wrong Answer" noise, repeated twice*

**Leonard** That's the wrong answer, I'm afraid, Nicola. It wasn't ten years ago, no.

**Nicola** Sorry, I—I don't know these sort of questions.

**Leonard** You mustn't say that, Nicola—must have a go, got to have a go at everything—the atmosphere beginning to get a little tense here—not to worry. Nothing to worry about. The year was—(*loudly*)—nineteen seventy-one. Of course. And our great thanks to Alderman Townshend for setting those questions. There are a lot more I may use later. The score is three points to Jane, and Nicola Davies is trailing behind with one point. Round Three now, folks, of the competition—which is carrying the greatest prize we have ever offered. My questions start here, girls, this is the first one. I'm going to say some words now—rather fast. I want you to tell me six of them. Ready, Nicola? I'm going to say them very fast, so be on the look-out. (*He fires the words out sharply*) Killer, Bottle, Junk, Rifle, Tune, Cheeseburger, Sickroom, Commercial, Knife, Disaster, Stereo, Limousine, Tube, Scar, Women's Lib, Cash Quickie, Needle, Platform, Pill, Dungaree, Snowball, Lump, Oil, Rape, Fire, Neddy, Assassin, Cardboard, Vegetable.

**Nicola** (*after a pause*) Assassin—Bottle—Needle . . . (*Pause; she begins to panic*)

**Leonard** That's only three, Nicola. Three.

*Nicola bites her lip*

**Nicola** Oil—Pill . . .

**Leonard** Have to hurry, you now. Something you ought to know about, being a woman.

**Nicola** (*after a pause*) Women's Lib.

*The bell rings loudly*

**Leonard** Well done, Nicola—well done. You now have two whole points, yes you do. (*Turning to Jane*) You thought I was going to do the same to you, Jane, didn't you?

**Jane** Yes.

**Leonard** But I'm not! (*Quickly*) Yes I am. Six please of the following. (*Very fast, even louder*) Chocolate, Wire, Tank, Plastic, Movie, Goldfish, Shares, Black, Judge, Union, Red, Grass, Steel, Sniper, Index, Trash, Hit, Disco, Chart-climber, Bomb, Cell, Beans, Hook, Barrier, Kite, T.V., Kennel, Motorway.

*Silence. Jane stares at him*

Six please, Jane, quickly . . .

**Jane** Chocolate—Motorway. (*Silence. She panics, her head in her hands*)

**Leonard** Quick, Jane, I have to hurry you, I'm afraid. (*Pause*) You're running out of time.

**Jane** (*panicking*) I don't know.

*A very loud "Don't Know" piercing noise*

**Leonard** I'm afraid you lose a life too, Jane. Jane loses a life! Both have lost a life now. Neck-and-neck. That's O.K., nothing to worry about. Doing very well, Jane. Nicola is sitting very still. This is the Competition of the Century. What I want you to do now, Jane, is in your own words, talk about a subject I will give you for *one whole* minute. And the subject is—Jane is smiling, she's straining at the leash—and the subject is—folks: "Why do I want to go to London?" if indeed you do. It is, of course, just one of the prizes of this competition. From now!

*Silence*

**Jane** I—I—want to go there—to London, because I've always . . . (*She stops*) Are you, are you allowed to repeat things, words?

**Leonard** Yes. You're allowed that. Come on.

**Jane** Because, because, I've always wanted to go there—and there's a shop in a street, I don't know which street, I saw it—this shop, late at night— when I was there once, in London, it's the only time I've ever been, and it was open at that time, I mean when shops aren't open, really, and so I wanted to go there, it had big posters in it, very, very big posters, some of pop-stars, some of politicians, and things, and one of a very fat woman with no clothes on—and it had flags all round, the shop did, I mean, and pictures, and names of streets, and souvenirs, cigarettes, and everything. And there was music coming out of it, very loud —right out into the street—be good to go and shop there. And I mean go and see things, that you know are famous, always been told about, and buy clothes, and look if you can't buy, because there are clothes shops everywhere, not like anywhere else, and see everything, all the night life—and I want——

*The bell goes*

**Leonard** Well done, Jane, thank you for that. That was very well done, wasn't it? Very good, Jane. Excellent. I'll give you three out of five for that. So now Jane has six whole points all to herself. "Six—points— Jane!" And now Nicola Davies, the subject for you is . . . (*Pause. He stares at her*)

**Nicola** Yes?

**Leonard** The subject on which you've got to talk for not less and not more than a minute is—wait for it—(*loudly*)—the last pop concert you went to.

*Pause*

**Nicola** The last—the last pop concert I went to . . . it was here in Leicester —(*she swallows*)—and Ross and the group were playing, and I queued to get in for a long time . . .

**Leonard** How long? How long did you queue for, Nicola?

**Nicola** (*completely thrown by his interruption*) I . . .

**Leonard** (*staring at her, more quietly, but matter-of-factly*) How long did you queue for, love?

**Nicola** I don't know, not . . .

*The "Don't Know" noise sounds, very loudly*

**Leonard** No, sorry. We don't count that! Rex is a little trigger-happy, watching out for don't knows. Come on, Nicola.

**Nicola** We queued for a day and a night, I think—it was a bit wet—you see, and the stone, the pavement, was very hard and cold, much harder than you think—because we slept there you see—it was all right and— and then a man came up, it was late you know then, dark and every- thing, and he'd come to sell us hot dogs and things, he came out there and he set up along the side of the queue, it was a very long queue, and then soon another—another came up out of the dark, and then there was another one, till there were lots and lots all along the line, really close. (*She looks up*)

**Leonard** (*staring at her, very close*) Go on, Nicola! Keep going. You're doing fine. You've got to keep going.

**Nicola** Oh! I thought it was enough.

**Leonard** I'm afraid it's not.

**Nicola** Oh—and—(*lost for words, she is extremely nervous*)—and then we went inside—and the concert—and it was them of course, and it was, you know—well it was all squashed—and some people rushed up and fought to get close—and there was a bit of biting, and that sort of thing, when they called out to us; they seemed a long way off—a very long way away, in their yellow and everything. They weren't very loud—but they made you feel—I felt something come up, you know, a little sort of . . . (*A second of slightly clenched feeling*)I got, you know, a bit worked up inside—they were moving very slowly on the stage like they'd been slowed down, made me feel strange—then they held things up, waved it at us, smiling and everything, they waved yellow scarves, Ross had a bit of yellow string he waved, I think it was, a bit of yellow rope, and I half wanted to kick the girl in front of me or something because I couldn't see; all the way through I had to look at her great back, pressed right up against it. I remember I half wanted to *get at it*. Move it. And I nearly dropped a ring. (*Pulling at her finger*) I'd been pulling at, put it on specially. (*Very nervously*) If you drop anything it's gone for ever, you know—can't bend down if you're standing—and if you drop yourself—then you'd be gone. When you rush out at the end, you can see all the millions of things that have been dropped shining all over the floor, nobody gets a chance to pick them up. And then it was finished—you know, the concert, and I came outside. It was cold, I was feeling a bit funny. Just walked along out there and I thought maybe I was bleeding. I looked but I wasn't. Some people like to be after a concert, but I wasn't.

*Pause. The bell rings*

**Leonard** Well done, Nicola! That was very, very nice. Fabulous, wasn't it, folks, fabulous. I'll give you five whole points for that. The very most I'm empowered to give. You now have seven points. Now what we want you to do is to sing a song, one of the Yellow Jacks' songs, and you must try not to get any of the words wrong. Rex knows the words, and he'll be watching . . .

*Nicola gets down off her chair, and moves away*

(*Sharply, still in his D.J. voice*) Where are you going, Nicola . . .

*Nicola half-turns. Leonard presses a button: covering music bursts out—the Beatles' "Sun King". He lowers the volume*

(*In a louder voice*) Where are you going?

**Nicola** (*turning to face him*) I was . . .

*Pause. The music plays*

**Leonard** Where on earth do you think you're going?

**Nicola** I—I wanted a glass of water.

**Leonard** (*calmly*) You don't walk away like that, do you—you can't leave the room, Nicola—we're in the middle of a competition, don't you realize . . .?

**Nicola** I know.

**Leonard** You've got to stay here, till we finish. (*Staring at her*) Haven't you . . .?

*She does not move*

Haven't you?

**Nicola** Yes, I—just wanted for a moment . . .

**Leonard** Come back here. We're on the air. Rex will get you something afterwards. (*He flicks a switch, the music dies*) We're here, never fear. Nicola's just had a little accident, went for a walkabout, in the MIDDLE of the Competition of the Century! Extraordinary, but she's back now. The question is, Nicola, Nicola, now, sing a song, and the song is Yellow Blues. Stand up, Nicola, will you. Nicola is standing up, and remember—the words must be right.

**Nicola** Yes.

*Pause. Nicola, standing, begins to sing a few words, then Rex makes a very loud "Wrong Answer" noise*

**Leonard** You've gone wrong, I'm afraid, Nicola. No points. Jane now, it's your turn. Your song is "I can give you love" by the Yellow Jacks. Like to stand up for it, Jane? Jane is standing up now! (*Quickly*) Rex is sweating, we're all sweating, the girls have been chewing their fingers, we've all chewed our fingers down to the bone; ready, Jane.

*Jane begins to sing; very quietly. She lasts longer than Nicola, but eventually the "Wrong Answer" buzzer goes*

Jane, you're wrong this time, I'm afraid. No score for that round at all. But I think I'm going to give her a point, because she lasted quite a long time. Well done, Jane. The girls have nice voices, don't they, pity we couldn't hear more of them. And now . . .

**Jane** Can I—can I change places, I can't really—I mean I can't concentrate here—because of the lights up there, and him up there. (*She looks upwards at Rex's box*)

**Leonard** (*quickly*) Jane's asked to change places, which is not in the rules! You can change places, we'll allow that, but what we'll do is—I'll ask you a question and then you both have to change places, run round the table, and the first one there, will have their microphone switched on, and will be able to try to answer. (*He looks at Nicola; smiles*) Ready to run, girls! And the question is—what were the names of the four Beatles—ready—steady—GO!

*They rush round the table, the long way*

(*As they run*) The girls are running now—running round—and it's Jane who's there first, Jane who gets there. Now the Beatles.

**Jane** (*she struggles*) Paul McCartney, John—John . . .

**Leonard** Have to give their surnames, too.

**Jane** John—and Ringo—John . . .

**Leonard** Have to hurry you.

**Jane** I can't—sorry.

**Leonard** You must know the names of the Beatles. (*Smiling*) Now, Nicola Davies, it's your big chance.

**Nicola** John—and Ringo—I can't remember the other one. (*Looking at him*) I don't know the other name.

*A very loud " Don't Know" noise*

**Leonard** Nicola's lost another life because of that. George Harrison, of course, was the answer. Nicola's only got one more life to her. Nothing to worry about. Now quick round we go again, we'll run before the question. Now! And they're off again, it doesn't take them long, panting and—(*loudly*)—round they go. That was about equal that time, I think—so we'll move on to the next question. (*Looking at Nicola*) To the final question of the Competition of the Century. And the great question is . . . (*Pause*) Wait for it: who can do the loudest scream for Ross and the boys? Who can do the very loudest scream? Right now, watch the windows, Rex! And you at home, watch your radio, because they may break your sets, in fact they probably *will break* them. And shatter all your ornaments. Nicola Davies is first. You do a scream for us now, Nicola. (*Silence*) Come on, Nicola, do a scream. That's all you have to do. (*In a funny voice*) I'm sure she can do it.

*Nicola sits still. Silence*

Come on, Nicola. You can do that, can't you, used to doing that.

*Nicola looks up, opens her mouth slightly, swallows hard, but makes no noise*

You can scream for the boys, can't you? A really loud one. That's why you're here, isn't it? (*Louder*) Isn't it! You haven't got long, Nicola.

*Nicola looks up and lets out a half-hearted scream*

There! She's done it! That wasn't a very loud one, was it, but now let's see what Jane can do. Ready, Jane, just a scream for them.

*Jane sits up straight, lets out a very, very long scream—which starts quietly, gets much louder than Nicola's, and very long*

Jane wins that. Jane wins that point. That is the end of the Competition of the Century, and what is THE SCORE?

**Rex** (*calling*) Very close, Leonard, very close indeed.

**Leonard** The scores are very close, so we are in fact going to invite *you* to cast *your* votes for the winner of our prize, going off with the Boys, to the centre of the universe, London Town. So ring us, on five-six-four-three-o, five-six-four-three-o, as quick as *you* can, as from NOW!

Just say "Jane" or "Nicola", that's all we require, if it's engaged, just dial again at once. And hurry, we're waiting, high up here, in our little box; put us out of our misery.

**Rex** (*shouting*) He's here! Ross has arrived!

**Leonard** And we've just heard, Ross is here, in the building, we've just felt the tremor go through it, and so, while we wait, butterflies swarming in our stomachs, let's have some proper music, a snatch of Rossini's *Thieving Magpie*, followed by a razor-sharp commercial or two.

*Leonard puts on the music. The girls sit as it plays loudly. There is a long pause—total stillness. Then Leonard cuts off the music*

(*To the girls*) You can get down now, girls, if you want. (*Calling*) Rex—get the girls a cup of tea. (*He looks at them*) Do you want a cup of tea?

*Jane nods*

*Mick enters, grinning happily*

**Nicola** (*quietly*) No thanks.

**Leonard** (*to Rex, his manner suddenly quiet, withdrawn*) Get Jane a cup of tea. And Nicola a glass of milk. You must have something, Nicola. And also wipe the spit off the mikes. (*Running his hand along the desk*) And wipe this, too, it's filthy.

**Rex** (*coming down from the box*) Len—that was . . . that was incredible.

**Leonard** (*quickly*) Was it? I can do without your comments.

**Mick** Yes, it was, Mr Brazil—really great.

**Rex** Yes, it was. It really was? It was a knockout. (*Smiling*) I've got Carol and everybody standing by. Everything's waiting.

*John enters*

**Leonard** (*turning*) What are you doing here?

**John** Tremendous, Leonard. (*To Rex*) Wasn't it? (*He looks at the girls*) You O.K., girls—bearing up? I've got some news for you now.

**Leonard** (*turning*) I wasn't expecting the news, I thought it had moved.

**John** (*smiling, unaware*) No, same schedule as always. Of course—life must go on. (*He smiles*)

*One telephone bell starts ringing faintly, off. It is answered*

**Rex** There we go. That's the first, they've started!

**Leonard** Get their drinks, Rex.

*Rex exits*

All right, girls, keep still where you are. Everyone keep still and don't speak. (*He moves to the mike and stops the record*) And to interrupt there! For, believe it or not, Big John is here with the local, national and international news.

*John sits, and begins to read the news, at first mundane items*

(*From the back wall, in a strong D.J. voice*) They call this news. (*Looking at Nicola*) Waste of time, isn't it?

*John continues reading*

(*In a louder voice*) Do they call this news?

*Telephone bells grow louder, more numerous. John starts reading more violent items. Suddenly Leonard moves over to the table and presses a button; music bursts out*

(*On the mike*) This is the Final here. Thank you, Big John, for reading the news for us. Now keep ringing. Keep those bells going ting-a-ling-a-ling, ring us, *please*. And while I wait I'll spin another circle of happiness and pour a little more Sugar over the City.

*The music continues*

**John** (*astonished*) I was only half-way through, Leonard.
**Leonard** That was enough news, wasn't it? I haven't spent a whole week whipping up the audience to lose them—let them drift away because of this. (*He picks up the news bulletin*) It can wait an hour, can't it. (*Loudly*) It's going to, anyway.
**John** (*picking up the bulletin*) All right, then—if that's what you want. (*smiling*) If *you* say so, first time that's ever happened. But since it's all going so tremendously—(*smiling*)—you can't let much get in your way right this moment, I can see that. Certainly I've never heard you in better form. Never. (*Smiling again*) Are you going to make a lot out of the announcement of the result, then . . . ?
**Leonard** (*sharply*) All right, John.

*Rex enters with the tea*

**John** (*smiling*) He's given me the chop, the news has got the chop for the first time.
**Rex** Yes, I heard. (*He gives the drinks to the girls*)
**Jane** Thank you. (*She tries to drink; it is very hot*)
**John** But worth it just this once, I think.
**Leonard** Look, get out of here, John, go on . . .

*John exits*

**Rex** Very soon now, girls, it'll be all over, won't it? Leonard.
**Leonard** (*turning back to him*) Yes?
**Rex** I wondered—I wondered if—*my minute . . .*?
**Leonard** Did you? (*He cuts the music*) Hello again—this is the control-room, competition week—Leicester, England. Jane and Nicola are a little tense, aren't they, a little pale, but they're smiling bravely. Jane's rose is dropping slightly, Nicola's is bulging . . .

**Rex** Leonard—my minute . . .

**Leonard** Young Rex is here—calling out to me—he's very eager to have a chance to speak to you—come here. (*He pulls Rex forward*) Here's your chance now, young Rex, how's it going?

**Rex** (*on the mike*) Hello—it's cracking along, Leonard, cracking. It's a great contest, isn't it, it's a fabulous contest, we're all agog back there—agog.

**Leonard** Are we? (*Staring at him*) I see, Rex.

**Rex** (*his voice getting louder, more confident*) The voting's very very close—the phones are jumping and ringing back there . . .

**Leonard** Jumping and ringing?

**Rex** Yes, Leonard—like they've got toothache. Want to hear it, folks? Want to hear them ringing, folks? (*He bends the mike towards the bells*)

**Leonard** We're not that posh anymore, are we?

**Rex** No—this is my voice now, Leonard—this is a Rex-type voice. And I just want to say hello to the listening millions with it. (*Quickly, smiling*) We really seem to have stirred the whole population, Leonard, like soup, we made callers of all ages back there, all sorts, from nine to ninety, all kinds of voices. The machines are over-loading back there—it's terrifying, it's wonderful.

**Leonard** The machines are so busy back there, they're going to explode.

**Rex** That's right, Leonard. Back there we really need six hands and six feet. (*He grins*) And six tongues! The girls are looking very happy at the moment, waiting for the result, didn't they do well—put up a great show.

**Leonard** We're making the most of things, aren't we, Rex—of our chances.

**Rex** That's right, Leonard—got to, haven't I. And it's a great feeling up here, a whale of a time—except the tension is killing me—stop the tension, Leonard—please—stop it, don't leave me, Len, don't leave me! You must stop the tension, it's killing me, my left foot's already gone dead.

**Leonard** You're a bit of a joker, aren't you, Rex. (*Louder*) A bit of a joker.

**Rex** That's what we all are, Leonard. That's why we're here, folks—sitting up here, that's how we've been made, Leonard, isn't that right?

**Leonard** A bit of an aper, aren't we, Rex?

**Rex** That's what I am, Leonard.

**Leonard** (*smiling*) And no questions asked.

**Rex** Of course not. No questions! That's all I can do, isn't it. I can't be any different. Play it again, Leonard.

**Leonard** (*staring at him*) Play it again, Rex. Rex likes the sound of his own voice, doesn't he?

**Rex** Yes! (*He laughs, standing over the mike*) I like the sound of my own voice all right. And I'd just like to say to the listening millions, it's intoxicating up here, folks. I'm flying with it, really flying. (*He looks at Leonard*) That's what we enjoy, folks, isn't it! No need to fear, Len and Rex are here. (*With a sudden change of tone: exuberantly, brilliantly*) And look—look at this, Leonard—see what's happening—I'm losing a little weight, Leonard, see, it's slipping off, it's starting to slip off, getting more now—see, reels and reels of fat are dropping off me on to the floor, they are! That's right, at this very moment, I wish you could see it, folks, Rex is losing the fat, it's just fallen off, whole streams of it coming away all over the studio, some's even gone over the controls, look at it, Leonard, have you ever seen anything like it—have you? But seriously, folks——

**Leonard** (*interrupting*) All right. That's enough, isn't it?

*Leonard pulls Rex away from the mike. Rex's hand still grips the mike—he has to be torn away*

Go and silence those bells, Rex. The girls can't wait any more.

**Rex** (*smiling broadly*) I'll go and silence them right away. (*Calling into the mike*) Last calls, please!

*Rex exits*

**Leonard** (*into the mike*) Rex has gone for the result—he has even dressed like me today, folks. Don't worry, girls, we're there now!

**Nicola** Where do you want me to sit?

**Leonard** Sit here, please, Nicola Davies. The girls are sitting by me now, I'm holding their hands, one each. They're sitting very straight, very correct, very calm. "They're tough girls you've got there, Brazil, they can take it!"

*Rex enters with an envelope*

Rex is bringing in the result—smiling proudly. That's a big envelope you're holding, Sound Engineer Rex.

**Rex** Yes, it is—Leonard.

**Leonard** (*his tone very quiet*) It has the word "WINNER" on the front in red ink. I'm opening the envelope, this is the moment we've hoped for. (*He looks at the card*) And the words on the card are—(*he glances at Nicola*)—Jane Harris! (*In a booming voice, repeating like a machine, fast*) Jane Harris is the winner, Jane Harris is the winner, Jane Harris is the winner. Let's have some applause. (*He brings up tumultuous applause on tape*) How do you feel, Jane? (*The applause dies away*)

**Jane** (*very quietly*) I feel—I feel—I feel—O.K. . . .

**Leonard** You must be very happy.

**Jane** (*quietly*) I am, yes.

**Leonard** How does Nicola feel? No hard feelings, I hope?

**Nicola** (*quietly*) I'm O.K.

**Leonard** Sound Engineer Rex is now going to take you, Jane, to where Ross is waiting. O.K., Rex, take her away.

**Rex** What? You mean me?

**Leonard** (*not looking at him, with papers on his desk*) Yes, you.

**Rex** (*quietly, watching him*) You're not really letting me handle it all, are you?

**Leonard** (*matter-of-factly*) Yes. It's what you want, isn't it?
**Rex** What? You're going to let me take her up—her up there, and deal with Ross and all that?
**Leonard** (*not looking up*) That's right. Go on.
**Rex** (*suddenly loudly*) Christ—that's incredible. That's really incredible! (*He takes Jane's hand, and pulls her towards the door*) Come on, you're coming with me. (*Stopping by the door*) That's fantastic of you, Leonard.
**Leonard** (*matter-of-factly*) There's no stopping you, anyway.
**Rex** (*looking at him*) I suppose not. (*With a slight smile*) Not now.
**Leonard** (*not looking up*) Go on, get out of my sight.
**Rex** (*smiling*) Right, Leonard.

*Rex waits for a moment, then exits with Jane*

*Leonard turns on music in the background, allowing himself to speak when he wants to*

**Leonard** Rex—an unimaginative kid, isn't he—but going places! (*He glances towards Nicola*) We'll be getting you a car, I hope, to run you back home. (*He is still very pent up, he brings the music up slightly, switches on to the air, the red light comes on, he sings along to the record. In his D.J. voice*) Any moment we'll be switching to Studio A, so wherever you are, whatever you're doing, *don't* go anywhere near the switch-off knob, because any minute now you'll be hearing the voice of Rex spreading out towards you—and just a reminder, the great group are going to Nottingham and Manchester, next Wednesday and next Saturday. (*He brings up the music*)

*Nicola touches the red lightbulb; Leonard continues looking towards her*

Don't touch that, it's hot.
**Nicola** Yeah—it is. (*She takes her hand away, and picks up her glass of milk*)
**Leonard** (*turning the red light on again*) I, Leonard Brazil, am taking a break now, a quick *snap*, a brrrreak. (*Calling*) Come in, Studio A, come in there. Hello—come in, Rex with the furry voice, it's all yours, then!
**Rex's Voice** (*on the intercom, booming over loudspeakers*) Thank you, Leonard for that introduction—Rex with the furry voice, here, we all liked that! And I have with me Jane, the lucky winner of the Competition of the Century, and the voice you've all been waiting for, in fact he's sitting in front of me and Jane right now, not only his voice, but *all of him*, the whole of the one and only, the greatest . . .

*Leonard clicks it off*

**Leonard** There.
**Nicola** Yes.

*Leonard gets up, and crumples a paper*

**Leonard** You O.K.?
**Nicola** Yes. (*She drops the full glass of milk in the middle of the stage; not having drunk any of it*)

**Leonard** Don't worry about that—it's a horrible mess in here anyway, isn't it?

**Nicola** (*staring round the studio*) Yes.

**Leonard** (*beginning to put on his jacket, and getting his papers together*) Disgusting leftovers everywhere—the junk that's been sent in here, been pouring in, crammed away in every corner and going bad, probably, it's a nasty room, this, isn't it—(*he rubs at the milk on the floor with his foot*) —this milk'll go grey-blue in a moment, hasn't been cleaned for months in here. (*Loudly*) It doesn't *look like* the nerve-centre of something, does it? Are you all right? (*He stands ready to go; he looks at her*)

**Nicola** Yes, I'm O.K.

**Leonard** Don't worry! We probably couldn't have let you win, anyway— could we. Because you won that L.P. It wouldn't have looked very good if you'd won both, would it. Might have smelt, as they say. (*Pause*) So you couldn't really have won.

**Nicola** (*quietly, blankly*) No—I know.

**Leonard** And you've done all right, haven't you, fought your way up into here for the final. You've been quite lucky really . . . (*Pause. Louder—as Nicola does not react*) You have, you know.

**Nicola** I know that, yes.

**Leonard** Good. Not much to see in London anyway. You mustn't believe what I've been saying about it, it's dead. (*Pause*) She's not going in *their* car, anyway, she's going in the second car of the convoy with the cook and the luggage. Half an hour's chat at midnight with them in a motorway café, and that's all she'll get. (*Pause*) Here—(*he picks up a tape*)—there's the tape of Ross we've been playing. You can have it if you want. (*Quickly changing*) No, I think it's got to be returned, they want to use it again. Stop us cutting him up. (*He changes his tone again and speaks suddenly loudly, straight to her*) You can't really like this shit, can you? Do you really, deep down inside, like this music?

*Nicola does not reply*

Do you?

**Nicola** A bit.

**Leonard** A bit—what does that mean? Either you do or you don't.

**Nicola** Yes, I do.

**Leonard** Right! (*Pause*) You know, Nicola, if, ten years ago, five years ago even—(*in a mocking voice*)—when things were very different—I'd been told that I'd be doing this job, playing this mindless milk chocolate pap endlessly to kids like you, I wouldn't have thought it remotely possible—(*loudly*)—not at all, it's not exactly what I imagined happening, not even in my greyest moments. It's extraordinary really that things have resulted in *you*! Do you know that?

*Nicola stands in front of him, silent*

I've been offered a job, too, Nicola, to do some more, a much, much bigger job, to chatter and gibber to many more people, lots of them, all waiting for it. And they want a decision. Quick answer!

*Nicola watches him; he stares straight at her*

This competition has been a great puller, you'll be pleased to know—
the most successful of all, you're the only lucrative corner of the market
left, that never fails, do you know that?

**Nicola** (*staring straight at him*) Yes.

**Leonard** All you have to do is just stop buying, don't you, as simple as
that, just stop, refuse to lap it up any more. Spit it out. *I mean that.*
(*Suddenly loudly*) Do you—understand a word I'm saying?

**Nicola** Yes—I do.

**Leonard** I don't often meet any of my audience this close. I picked you
out, do you know that, homed in on you. I picked out that voice, that
slightly dead, empty sort of voice. Picked it out as Miss Average—
which in fact you probably are not, and I followed that flat voice, each
announcement was aimed at it.

**Nicola** Oh, I see . . .

**Leonard** I let it get through each stage, let you clamber up here, because
I wanted to see it—*meet you*, face you. (*Loudly*) And now you're here.

**Nicola** (*quietly*) Yes.

**Leonard** (*louder*) Is monosyllables all I'm going to get?

**Nicola** Yes.

**Leonard** What did you think of the competition, then?

*Pause*

Come on . . .

**Nicola** I don't know. (*She looks straight at him, coldly*) I don't know what
I thought of it . . .

**Leonard** (*abrasively*) Got a little out of hand—though it'll have sounded
all right down there. Is that how you'd put it?

**Nicola** I don't know.

**Leonard** There was just a touch of revenge, don't you think—I must want
a little revenge—I glanced at you before the first question and saw that
stare, that blank, infuriatingly vacant gaze, and then it just happened.
I wanted to see just how far I *could push you*, how much you'd take—I
was hoping you'd come back—that something would come shooting
back, that you'd put up a fight, Nicola. Why didn't it? Why don't you?
(*Suddenly very loudly*) What's the matter with all you kids now—what
is it? Come on, answer me, you know what I'm talking about, you're
not a small child, you know what I mean.

*Pause*

(*Abrasively*) Are you going to talk to me?

**Nicola** No.

**Leonard** Why not?

**Nicola** I—(*a slight pause*)—I don't want to.

**Leonard** You don't want to. (*Pause*) Come here. (*Loudly*) You're not
hoping to get away with that, are you? Come here—come on, Nicola.
(*He pulls her up to him and holds her by the arm*) There. After all, I

brought you up here for this meeting. (*He stares down at her with a slight smile*) What are you going to do now, Nicola?

*Pause. She does not move*

You don't even look startled! Nothing!
**Nicola** No.
**Leonard** (*shouting*) COME ON!—(*holding her by the arm in front of him he shakes her violently*)—had no effect on you at all.
**Nicola** (*slightly louder*) No.
**Leonard** (*still holding her*) You almost feel, Nicola Davies—as if you're from another planet, do you know that?

*No answer. He turns*

I would give you a lift, love, but I'm going for a walk. Got to work things out. (*Very matter-of-factly*) What are we going to do, *love*. (*He looks about her*) Are you all right? (*Looking about the studio*) You won't do anything silly—will you? No. (*He flicks on a switch, Ross's voice booms out*) There!

*Leonard exits*

**Ross's Voice** (*on the speakers*) The receptions we've been getting have been fabulous, *really* fabulous. You know, really warm, and we've had no bother, no trouble of any kind, everything's been calm and nice——

*Nicola picks up her bag*

—which should put a sock in all those critics who've written about us. And to see those faces in the front row, they're always a special sort of face in the front row, I don't know how to describe it, but in the front row the faces are always different.

*Nicola fastens her bag and moves out of the Studio*

**Rex's Voice** (*on the speakers*) I know what you mean. I've noticed that myself.

*Nicola moves into the shop area*

**Ross's Voice** (*on the speakers*) And also English front rows are very different, totally different in a funny kind of way, from American front rows.

*Ross's voice fades into the noise of a loud hum from the shop's refrigerator, as the Lights in the Studio fade to a Black-out*

### SCENE 8

*The Supermarket*

*Nicola stands facing Susan, who is standing opposite her holding a dustpan and brush. The shop has closed its doors for the evening: silent and dark except for a light shining up from inside the refrigerator*

**Susan** (*by the refrigerator*) Why are you so late? I wondered if you'd show up at all.

**Nicola** I got delayed.

**Susan** I've been hanging around for a long time. Everybody's gone, almost. Had to do this corner all by myself, and there was lots of it, bloody place. Done most of it now anyway. So you lost, didn't you.

**Nicola** Yes—that's right—I lost. (*Pause. She smiles slightly*) You're right. (*She turns, and bites her lip. Her mood is one of controlled violence*)

**Susan** You O.K.?

**Nicola** Yes, I'm O.K. (*Louder*) I'm all right. (*Pause*) Did you hear it?

**Susan** Yes, some of it.

**Nicola** (*suddenly loudly*) What do you mean, *some* of it?

**Susan** (*surprised*) No, I heard it. Quite a lot.

**Nicola** (*savagely and very loudly*) Why didn't you hear all of it? (*Shouting*) YOU SHOULD HAVE HEARD IT ALL! ALL OF IT! (*Pause; suddenly matter-of-factly*) You'd only have been able to tell if you'd seen it. Been there. (*Pause*) What did you think?

**Susan** You were O.K.

*Nicola pulls a packet of fish-fingers out of the refrigerator and lets it drop*

**Nicola** O.K.?

**Susan** Ought to have won, really.

**Nicola** Yes, I know. (*Pause*) It was very hot up there.

**Susan** They really put you through it.

**Nicola** Yeah—they did. (*With a sudden smile*) Hey, look at that. (*She pulls the leg of the dummy out of her bag*) It fell off! That's what they made me make . . .

**Susan** That's right. (*Smiling*) Should do it to it all.

*Nicola drops the bag with the dummy in it into the refrigerator. She smiles*

**Nicola** Could put it in here, watch it go hard, freeze it, then pull it to bits easily. (*She pulls out the bag and stares into the refrigerator*) Not much left in there, is there. (*Suddenly louder*) Not much left!

**Susan** (*bewildered by Nicola's aggression*) Yes.

**Nicola** (*quickly*) It was interesting really seeing him, seeing the D.J., there, that was interesting! (*Suddenly louder, quite clenched*) It was all interesting—*everything.* (*Pulling more packets of fish-fingers out of the refrigerator*) Lot of these left, anyway.

*As they talk, Nicola keeps pulling more packets out, undoing packets and dropping them*

**Susan** You going to queue for the concert?

**Nicola** Don't think so. I don't want to. They're all right, I s'pose. But I'm not going this time.

**Susan** I might go. I don't know.

**Nicola** Anyway, it's not worth it. It really isn't! (*She holds the bag very tightly, with the dummy inside, clenched violence inside her*)

**Susan** Are you *all right*, Nicola? Not ill or anything?

**Nicola** (*louder*) Yuh, I'm fine. I told you. There's nothing wrong with me. (*She glances behind her*) It's all different here when it's dark. (*By the refrigerator again*) Nobody's watching. We could throw all this out if we wanted. And all the rest, spread it all over the shop—first thing they'd see Monday morning. They'd never know who it was.

**Susan** (*with excited, uninhibited violence*) We can do the whole place, if we wanted, the cameras are off, dead, it wouldn't take long. The shelves come down easily, just fall off, and the stacks of cans, just have to pull one and millions come down, all pouring down. Could make them all do that. We could finish the whole place. It would be very easy really . . .

**Nicola** Yes. (*Loudly*) *Tear through it if we wanted*. But it's not worth it really. I don't think it's worth it. Maybe next time. We'll see next time. (*Savagely*) I'll see next time.

**Susan** What do you mean, next time?

**Nicola** (*biting her lip hard*) I don't know, I don't know, do I?

**Susan** You're in a funny mood, aren't you?

**Nicola** (*tightly*) Yeah, that's right. I s'pose I am.

**Susan** You are—never seen you like this . . .

**Nicola** No, that's right.

*The distant noise of a radio voice is heard*

**Susan** Sssh—hear that—listen to that.

**Nicola** What?

**Susan** There—hear it now? That talking, that voice . . .

**Nicola** Yes.

**Susan** Where's it coming from—somewhere near—very near. Can't see.

**Nicola** Don't know—but it's him all right.

*The Lights fade to a Black-out*

SCENE 9

*The Studio*

*Leonard is standing over the controls: he fades down his own noise*

**Leonard** Hello. That was, of course, L.B.'s jingle, and this is a very special moment, for which I'm standing, I really am, all alone in this studio, standing above the controls, which are hot and steaming. Thank you to Rex for his first great solo over the air. Very smooth, very good. That was a Rex-type interview. (*His tone changes*) I've got to tell you something now which is quite a surprise, because today I was offered a very big job in London, with the very splendid Capitol Radio—and they offered me a lot of money and a large, large audience, in London,

the capital of this fine country of ours, and a fat programme, to do my
very own thing. They offered me this job earlier today. "We must have
you" they said. "We must have him." And I have thought about it.
(*Smiling, loudly, jubilantly*) And I have accepted their offer! Yes I have.
I'm going there. I, Len Brazil, Lennnnnn Brazil, am leaving you for
Capital Land, London! I hear it'll need four people to fill my job here,
which is nice, but I'm going to London where all the action is—where
I'll be giving a few jokes and all the hits and more, all the sounds and
more, all the luck and more, where I'll be seeing us through our present
troubles, obliterating the bad times—that's a Big Word, and remembering
the good times, oh yes, and letting people remember and letting them
forget. Drowning all our sorrows, yes I said drowning, till we're emerging
out of the clouds, of course. And now I hope my voice is reaching out,
spreading to the four corners of our area—across the whole city—
through the blackness, swooping into cars on the motorway and down
chimneys, and through brick walls and across pylons. Over the whole
domain, until it reaches you. Because I want to say, I'm sorry, folks,
but there it is. I'm sorry to leave you, folks; but it's how I've always
wanted things, of course—what I wanted! Don't spit on the animals,
I'm speaking to *you* now, I am, remember this, when you're in London,
don't forget to give us a ring, want to hear from you, over the air, at
the very least don't forget to tune in. Yes tune in! What are you doing,
Brazil—tell us—what on earth is he doing—He's saying *Good-bye* and
don't *forget*. We're going to lick it, of course we will. No need to worry,
no need to be sad. Shout that out. So tune in—I said tune in. Because
I'll take your mind off things, oh yes. I will. (*He brings in music—
"Days", by the Kinks*) Hear that—some music! Music for Len's fare-
well. Tune in, I said. (*Very loudly*) TUNE IN! This is how we like it.
I've got some great times for you, oh yes. You know I'll never let you
down. That was Competition Week. This is Len Brazil. Be seeing you.

*The Lights fade to a Black-out, and—*

*the* CURTAIN *falls*

# FURNITURE AND PROPERTY LIST

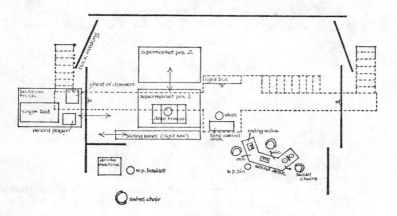

### SCENES 1–5

*On stage:* STUDIO:
>> Sound desk. For contents see special plan.
>> 4 swivel chairs
>> Drinks machine. *Below it:* wastepaper-basket
>> Stool (under Control Box)
>> Cupboard (under Control Box). *In it:* reels of loose tape, boxes
>> *On Gallery:* Control Box. For contents see special plan
>> *On movable wall:* various coloured posters, pop groups, etc.

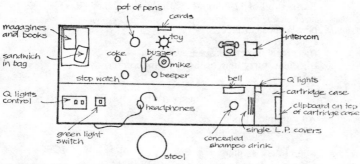

Rex's box setting, Scenes 1–5 & 6–9

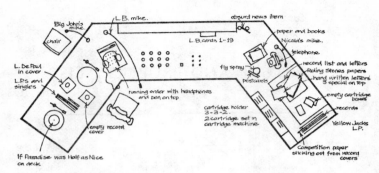

L.B. desk setting, Scenes 1–5

**SUPERMARKET:**
Large deep-freeze or refrigerator. *In it:* packaged and canned foods
Moving watching-eye T.V. camera suspended from ceiling
Loudspeaker for radio music, Leonard's voice, etc.

**BEDROOM:**
Divan bed and bedding
Shelves and cupboards round and at head of bed. *On and in them:*
    magazines, cans and packets of food, tin of paint and brush, make-
    up, ornaments and other oddments
Chest-of-drawers. *In them:* clothing
*On walls:* posters of pop stars
*Under bed:* magazines, packets of food, posters, Nicola's dummy—in
    pieces
*On proscenium arch:* telephone (for use in bedroom and supermarket
    scenes

*Off stage:*   4 sacks full of postcards **(Mick)**
              Brief-case, news sheets **(Big John)**
              Trolley with "bribes"—including watch, packet of cheese, photo-
                 graphs, T shirt, walking-stick, socks, cake, assorted parcels **(Mick)**
              Barrow full of 12 dummies with cards attached **(Rex)**

*Personal:*   **Nicola:** postcard
              **Leonard:** watch
              **Rex:** black notebook, pen, watch
              **Big John:** furry mascot, box of peppermints

SCENES 6–9

*Strike:*   All dummies, trolley, etc.
            Tape boxes, loose tape

*Set:*      Sound desk as plan
            Cheese puffs and sandwich in BEDROOM

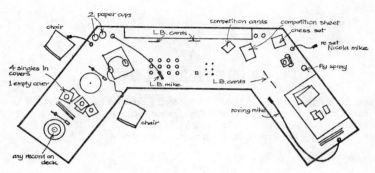

L.B. desk setting, Scenes 6–9


*Off stage:*  Tray with letters, postcards, small parcels **(Rex)**
Tray with bottle of wine, 3 glasses, 2 roses with pins **(Rex)**
Tray with teapot and tea bag, cup, saucer, cup with sliced lemon, 2 paper cups—one half-full of milk, one with tea bag, thermos water-jug, teaspoon **(Rex)**
"Winner" envelope and card **(Rex)**
Bag with dummy inside, leg separate **(Nicola)**
Dustpan and brush **(Susan)**

# LIGHTING PLOT

Property fittings required: STUDIO: coloured lights and effects on Sound Desk and Control Box. SUPERMARKET: strip lighting, light in deep freeze. BEDROOM: lampholder with detachable shade
Interior. A Studio, Bedroom, Supermarket department

SCENES 1–5

| | | |
|---|---|---|
| *To open:* | Studio lighting up | |
| *Cue* 1 | **Leonard:** "We're off." | (Page 8) |
| | *Fade to Black-out* | |
| *Cue* 2 | *Song on radio:* "Liptons make the going great!" | (Page 8) |
| | *Snap on Supermarket lighting* | |
| *Cue* 3 | **Leonard:** "I'm waiting for you, aren't I?" | (Page 13) |
| | *Fade to Black-out* | |
| *Cue* 4 | When ready | (Page 13) |
| | *Fade up Studio lighting* | |
| *Cue* 5 | **Leonard:** *"I don't like competitions!"* | (Page 19) |
| | *Fade to Black-out* | |
| *Cue* 6 | When ready | (Page 19) |
| | *Fade up Bedroom lighting* | |
| *Cue* 7 | **Nicola:** "It's finished." | (Page 23) |
| | *Fade to Black-out* | |
| *Cue* 8 | When ready | (Page 23) |
| | *Fade up Studio lighting* | |
| *Cue* 9 | **Leonard:** "I wasn't going to do that." | (Page 31) |
| | *Fade to Black-out* | |

SCENES 6–9

| | | |
|---|---|---|
| *To open:* | Black-out | |
| *Cue* 10 | After song ends | (Page 32) |
| | *Fade up Bedroom lighting* | |
| *Cue* 11 | **Susan:** "Now you're ready." | (Page 35) |
| | *Fade to Black-out* | |
| *Cue* 12 | When ready | (Page 35) |
| | *Fade up Studio lighting* | |
| *Cue* 13 | **Ross:** ". . . from American front rows." | (Page 57) |
| | *Fade to Black-out* | |
| *Cue* 14 | When ready | (Page 57) |
| | *Fade up Supermarket, lit only by light in freezer* | |
| *Cue* 15 | **Nicola:** ". . . it's him all right." | (Page 59) |
| | *Cross-fade to Studio lighting* | |
| *Cue* 16 | **Leonard:** "Be seeing you." | (Page 60) |
| | *Fade to Black-out* | |

# MUSIC PLOT

(Listed here are the records used in the West End production—current Top Twenty tunes may be substituted to keep the production up-to-the-minute)

Scene 1—Studio:
"Paradise is half as nice"                        Amen Corner
"No Honestly"                                  Lynsey De Paul
"Gonna sell a million"                               Lyn Paul
Special Leicester Sound Jingle
"The Proud One" (*slowed down*)                      Osmonds
"NaNa is the saddest word" (*slowed down*)      The Stylistics
Special Competition Loop

Scene 2—Supermarket:
"Viva L'Espagna"                                      Sylvia
"Long Haired lover from Liverpool"             Jimmy Osmond
"Rodriges Guitar Concerto"   Manuel & Music of the Mountains
Special Competition Loop

Scene 3—Studio:
"Sweet Talking Guy"                                 Chiffones
Special Leicester Sound Jingle
Special "Holiday" Commercial
Special "Bubblemint" Commercial
"Satisfaction"                                 Rolling Stones
Special News Jingle
"Walk in the Black Forest"                   Horst Jankowski
Special Competition Loop

Scene 4—Bedroom:
"W.O.L.D."                                       Harry Chapin
"Whole Lot of Loving going on"
"Raindrops are falling on my head"               B. J. Thomas
"Happy to be on an Island"                      Demis Roussos

Scene 5—Studio:
"Hey Bulldog"                                        Beatles
"See Emily Play"                                  Pink Floyd
"Whiter Shade of Pale"                          Procul Harum
"Baby Face"                                        Babyface
"20001/Zarathrustra"           Royal Philharmonic & Karajan
Special Competition Loop
"Whole Lotta Love"                              Led Zepplin

Scene 6—Bedroom:
Special Version of "I can give you love"       Nicola & Susan

# EFFECTS PLOT

NOTE:     All music and other sounds from **Leonard Brazil**'s desk are worked by
          the actor's use of the practical equipment on it

## SCENES 1–5

*Cue* 1     At start of Scene 2                                              (Page 8)
            *Commercial on radio in Supermarket, followed by back-*
            *ground music until* **Leonard**'s *voice takes over*
*Cue* 2     **Susan:** "Hurry!"                                             (Page 12)
            *Loud engaged tone from phone*
*Cue* 3     **Nicola:** "Ssssh!"                                            (Page 12)
            *Loud engaged tone*
*Cue* 4     **Nicola** dials a third time                                   (Page 12)
            *Very loud telephone "pips"*
*Cue* 5     At start of Scene 4                                             (Page 19)
            *Background music from Nicola's radio*

## SCENES 6–9

*Cue* 6     **Nicola:** ". . . more than anything else."                    (Page 33)
            *Telephone rings*
*Cue* 7     **Leonard:** ". . . oily sod Johnson, he——"                     (Page 35)
            *Telephone rings*
*Cue* 8     **Leonard:** ". . . life must go on."                           (Page 50)
            *Telephone rings off-stage, and is answered*
*Cue* 9     **Leonard:** "Do they call this news?"                          (Page 51)
            *Telephone bells louder, becoming numerous and*
            *continuing*
*Cue* 10    **Nicola:** ". . . want me to sit?"                             (Page 53)
            *Reduce telephone bells to silence*

Scene 7—Studio:
    Special Competition Loop
    Special Commercial Music
    "The Man who sold the World"              David Bowie
    "Sun King"                                      Beatles
    Rossini's "Thieving Magpie Overture"    Berlin Philharmonic
    "We do it"                                 R. &. J. Stone
    "Oh by Jingo"                                        ?

Scene 8—Supermarket
    None

Scene 9—Studio:
    "Behind Blue eyes"                          The Who
    Special Leicester Sound Jingle
    "Days"                                      The Kinks

*The following statement concerning the use of music is printed here on behalf of the
Performing Right Society Ltd, by whom is was supplied*

The permission of the owner of the performing right in copyright music must be
obtained before any public performance may be given, whether in conjunction
with a play or sketch or otherwise, and this permission is just as necessary for
amateur performances as for professional. The majority of copyright musical
works (other than oratorios, musical plays and similar dramatico-musical works)
are controlled in the British Empire by the Performing Right Society Ltd, Copyright House, 29–33 Berners Street, London W1.

    The Society's practice is to issue licences authorizing the use of its repertoire to
the proprietors of premises at which music is publicly performed, or, alternatively,
to the organizers of musical entertainments, but the Society does not require pay-
ment of fees by performers as such. Producers or promoters of plays, sketches,
etc., at which music is to be performed, during or after the play or sketch, should
ascertain whether the premises at which their performances are to be given are
covered by a licence issued by the Society, and if they are not, should make applica-
tion to the Society for particulars as to the fee payable.

MADE AND PRINTED IN GREAT BRITAIN BY
LATIMER TREND & COMPANY LTD, PLYMOUTH
MADE IN ENGLAND

YELLOW BLUES

*slowly*

Well you know the blues that make you sad the blues that make you blue

If you're feeling kind-a bad I've got the blues for you

*bouncy*

Sing the yel-low blues    Sing the yel-low blues

And the yel-low blues    Will make you smile A-

gain sing the yel-low    blues

I CAN GIVE YOU LOVE

*slow ballad*    *lilting beat*

I'll give you April    showers    Daff-o-dils in Ma- -y

I'll give you June-time flowers    Ro-ses ev-ery da- -y

Don't you think that May be    you could be my ba- by    my

sweet little ang-el from a - bove 'cause I can give you    love * (yes I can)

I can give you    love * (be your man) be my lit-tle    ba- by Don't you think that

May-be I can give you love    I loved you in Dec - em - ber ———

*\* These lines are sung by another singer on the record at the begining of Act Two, but not
by Jane in the competition. She leaves a pause, and beats time nervously with her foot*